Cambridge Elements

Elements in Economics of European Integration
edited by
Nauro F. Campos
University College London and ETH-Zürich

THE HAPPINESS REVOLUTION IN EUROPE

Richard Ainley Easterlin†
University of Southern California
Kelsey James O'Connor
STATEC Research

Shaftesbury Road, Cambridge CB2 8EA, United Kingdom

One Liberty Plaza, 20th Floor, New York, NY 10006, USA

477 Williamstown Road, Port Melbourne, VIC 3207, Australia

314–321, 3rd Floor, Plot 3, Splendor Forum, Jasola District Centre, New Delhi – 110025, India

103 Penang Road, #05–06/07, Visioncrest Commercial, Singapore 238467

Cambridge University Press is part of Cambridge University Press & Assessment, a department of the University of Cambridge.

We share the University's mission to contribute to society through the pursuit of education, learning and research at the highest international levels of excellence.

www.cambridge.org
Information on this title: www.cambridge.org/9781009493659

DOI: 10.1017/9781009493697

When citing this work, please include a reference to the DOI 10.1017/9781009493697

First published 2025

A catalogue record for this publication is available from the British Library.

ISBN 978-1-009-49365-9 Hardback
ISBN 978-1-009-49370-3 Paperback
ISSN 2634-0763 (online)
ISSN 2634-0755 (print)

The Happiness Revolution in Europe

Elements in Economics of European Integration

DOI: 10.1017/9781009493697
First published online: February 2025

Richard Ainley Easterlin†
University of Southern California

Kelsey James O'Connor
STATEC Research

Author for correspondence: Kelsey James O'Connor,
kelsey.oconnor@statec.etat.lu

Abstract: There is now a Happiness Revolution to go along with the earlier Industrial and Demographic Revolutions. The Happiness Revolution is captured using people's happiness scores, as reported in public surveys, whereas the earlier revolutions are reflected by economic production (such as GDP) and life expectancy. Increases in happiness are chiefly due to social-science welfare policies that alleviate people's foremost concerns – those centering on family life, health, and jobs. This Element traces the course of the Happiness Revolution throughout Europe since the 1980s when comprehensive and comparable data on people's happiness first became available. Which countries lead and which lag? How is happiness distributed – are the rich happier than the poor, men than women, old than young, native than foreign born, city than countryfolk? How has the COVID-19 pandemic impacted happiness? These are among the questions addressed in this Element. This title is also available as Open Access on Cambridge Core.

Keywords: happiness, Europe, economic growth, welfare-state programs, subjective well-being

ISBNs: 9781009493659 (HB), 9781009493703 (PB), 9781009493697 (OC)
ISSNs: 2634-0763 (online), 2634-0755 (print)

Contents

Foreword: Remembering Professor Richard Easterlin

Richard Easterlin was one of the world's most creative social scientists.

As I have argued elsewhere, to understand Professor Easterlin properly, if you never met him, the central thing to grasp is that he was an intellectual iconoclast. He was arguably even perhaps the iconoclast's iconoclast, because his ideas were conceptually rebellious within fields of study that in some cases were themselves, I suppose, analytically rebellious. Those fields included the economics of happiness and the statistical study of people's fertility decisions.

I would say that the main task of universities is to foster and debate revolutionary ideas. That is why they seek to employ the rare men and women who are extreme iconoclasts.

Richard Easterlin's most remarkable idea turns much of standard economics upside down (and remains disputed by large numbers of conventional thinkers). It is the argument, now famously called the Easterlin Paradox (Easterlin, 1974), that as nations grow richer they do not grow happier. This is either wrong or one of the most profound notions ever put forward by a researcher in any field of academia. In either case, that disconcerting proposition and its associated evidence has in principle to be faced by each prime minister, finance minister, and president on our planet. My view is that over the next hundred years they will eventually have to, so we will see such a conceptual confrontation. Climate change may hasten the uncomfortable reckoning.

There was nothing deliberately obdurate or willful about the Easterlinian choice to say things that others had never said. He simply saw the world differently – more shrewdly, more humanly, more humanely. I do not know why he was like this. Perhaps the roots of such things lie in childhood and upbringing; perhaps they are provoked by innate personality. A glance at his CV shows that this precious ability began decades before I first met him, which was at the conference "Economics and The Pursuit of Happiness", Nuffield College Oxford, 11 – 12 February 2000.

Dick [as he was called by friends] Easterlin went so strongly against the intellectual herd that it required decades for his most fundamental ideas to take hold. The famous 1974 paper (Easterlin, 1974), which he told me he found impossible to publish in a regular refereed economics journal, ends with the following sentences: "If the view suggested here has merit, economic growth does not raise a society to some ultimate state of plenty. Rather, the growth process itself engenders ever-growing wants that lead it ever onward." In my view, this has the ring of truth. Since those words were written, I think it might be fair to say that such judgments, expressed in a variety of ways, and often without formal statistical evidence, have become relatively common.

Since early 1974, material riches have been spread, especially throughout a fortunate elite minority, but also in part across the majority of citizens too, at least within the modern industrialized nations. However, do we see rejoicing and widespread contentment in a consistent way? Concerns about mental health and work overload are now everywhere in the media and in informal discussions around dinner tables in prosperous countries. That was not a feature of life in 1974, nor even in the early 2000s. Formal study of mental-health scores through time are also not encouraging. Richard Easterlin would say, and I think correctly, that humans find it almost impossible to feel happier as they get richer if they see all those around them becoming richer. People, although they do not mean to do it, are intrinsically relativistic in how they feel and do their social comparisons.

Today – and here regression equations are not needed – we are living in a visible and continuing laboratory experiment. All readers will be familiar with it.

The BMWs get faster, larger (despite shrinking family sizes), more glamorous. Newspapers like the Financial Times and the Economist carry advertising photographs of intricate men's watches, ones that sell for prices that could buy an apartment in most of the world's cities, and are purchased by individuals who all carry mobile phones that tell the time anyway. Is the great tide of economic progress in the advantaged nations leading self-evidently to increasingly cheerful, carefree, smiling citizens?

The second main concept for which Dick Easterlin is known is a contribution to demography. It is often called the Easterlin Hypothesis or Easterlin Effect. Large cohort size, the argument goes, leads to worse circumstances for the citizens born in those cohorts. Low relative status – in terms of economic prosperity for the individuals, especially when psychologically compared to that of their parents – then alters how those individuals behave. They have fewer babies. They marry later. They display signs of alienation. The ups and downs of birth rates in this way have a foundational role, years later, in how well a society functions.

I miss Dick Easterlin for his gentleness and his intellectual brilliance. His ideas will live on.

Andrew Oswald
Professor of Economics and Behavioural Science,
University of Warwick, UK

1 Introduction

In the modern era, there are three great breakthroughs in the human condition. The first, starting around 1800, is the Industrial Revolution, which continues even today to totally transform people's *objective* living conditions – their food, clothing, shelter, and the like. The second, the Demographic Revolution, began in the latter part of the nineteenth century, and is vastly improving people's observed health and length of life – many infectious diseases have been conquered and life expectancy at birth has doubled. The third is the newly emerging Happiness Revolution, which is advancing people's *subjective* satisfaction with their lives – with their *feelings* of well-being. Already, the governments of nine European countries use measures of well-being in their decision-making process (Mahoney, 2023).

These three revolutions are due, at bottom, to the emergence and evolution of modern science since the seventeenth century – the Industrial Revolution, primarily to the rise of the natural sciences; the Demographic Revolution, to the subsequent development of the life sciences; and the Happiness Revolution, to the more recent birth of the social sciences. Western and Northern Europe, the cradle of modern science, is the leader in all three revolutions. Each of the three revolutions has a distinctive marker of progress – real GDP per capita for the Industrial Revolution, life expectancy at birth for the Demographic Revolution, and subjective well-being (SWB) for the Happiness Revolution.

1.1 Measuring Subjective Well-Being

But what exactly is subjective well-being? We need to define it before we can delve into the details of the Happiness Revolution. Subjective well-being is the technical term for people's feelings of well-being or sense of happiness. Subjective well-being data are obtained in nationally representative surveys in which questions are asked like "Taking all things together, how would you say things are these days – would you say you are very happy, pretty happy, or not too happy?"[1] The question uses the clauses, "taking all things together" and "these days" to frame the question in such a way that respondents *evaluate* their life in a broader context, and do not simply report their current *feelings*. While the question is about happiness, it elicits more than an emotion; it elicits what we call *evaluative* subjective well-being.

Evaluative subjective well-being is one of three forms of subjective well-being. The two others are affective and eudemonic subjective well-being. Affective metrics typically include multiple measures of positive and negative

[1] One of the initial public poll inquiries regarding people's feelings of well-being, it was first asked around the middle of the twentieth century (Bradburn, 1969), has since been included in surveys all over the world, and is still an oft-used query.

feelings such as joy, cheerfulness, worry, sadness, and anger. Eudaimonia is the least clear conceptually and least commonly measured across the Organisation for Economic Co-operation and Development (OECD) (Mahoney, 2023). It comes from Aristotle, who described it as living a good, virtuous, life (Aristotle, 2012). These days we also associate it with purpose or meaning, or psychological functioning (Martela and Ryan, 2023). While each of the three forms is distinct, they are also closely related to each other. In this Element, we focus on evaluative measures because they have been better harmonized across countries (Mahoney, 2023), economists generally prefer them, and compared to affect measures, evaluative subjective well-being is more stable and better predicted by one's life circumstances (Helliwell and Wang, 2012).

Evaluative subjective well-being questions are now asked all around the world, with slight variations across surveys. In 1973, all European Union member states started asking about life satisfaction on a four-point scale. Soon after in 1981, the European Values Study (EVS) began, which asks: "All things considered, how satisfied are you with your life as a whole these days?" with integer response options from 1 (=Dissatisfied) to 10 (=Satisfied). The Gallup World Poll (GWP), initiated in 2005, uses a "Best–Worst" question (termed here "Best Possible Life") in which people rate their lives on a ladder with steps numbered from 0 to 10, where 0, at the bottom of the ladder, equals the worst possible life in their view, and 10, the top step, equals the best.[2] The Gallup World Poll covers more than 160 countries representing more than 99 percent of the world's population.

All of these questions about feelings of well-being, in which people are asked to evaluate their lives, yield quite similar results about long-term trends and differences in subjective well-being among countries and among subgroups of the population within a country. Hence, these measures are typically used interchangeably as indicators of evaluative subjective well-being. This Element principally uses the last two measures – EVS "Life Satisfaction" and GWP "Best Possible Life" – as the measures of subjective well-being. We refer to them both by the less cumbersome and more user-friendly term, "happiness."

1.2 Are Happiness Measures Meaningful?

In surveys of subjective well-being, clearly, each individual responds based on his or her own notion of happiness, and these notions could conceivably differ widely from one person to the next. If, then, one puts together the answers of the respondents in a nationally representative survey and computes an "average" value of happiness, as is commonly done and done here, is the result meaningful?

[2] The Best Possible Life scale is referred to technically as the Cantril Self-Anchoring Striving Scale Cantril, (1965).

There are three ways of answering this question, and each yields an affirmative result. The first is by appeal to authority. Here, for example, is the answer of the twenty-five-member *Commission on the Measurement of Economic Performance and Social Progress* appointed in 2008 by then-president Nicolas Sarkozy of France to suggest better measures of social progress than GDP.

> Research has shown that it is possible to collect meaningful and reliable data on *subjective* as well as *objective* well-being . . . [T]he types of questions that have proved their value within small-scale and unofficial surveys should be included in larger scale surveys undertaken by official statistical offices. (Stiglitz et al., 2009, p. 16 emphasis added)

The Commission members were almost entirely leading economists and included five Nobel Prize winners (now six). They hailed from an era when economists were trained in the view that measures of one's observable external circumstances, especially income, are sufficient to assess well-being, and that self-reports of feelings such as happiness should be summarily dismissed. The more recent judgment quoted earlier that personal statements about one's feelings of well-being are meaningful represents a revolutionary change in the attitude of the economics discipline – a willingness to pay attention to what people say, not just observe what they do.

A second way to assess the meaningfulness of happiness responses is by considering what people report when asked what makes them happy. Given the open-ended nature of the happiness questions, one might suppose that responses on the sources of happiness might be widely different from one person to the next. But, in fact, the responses are amazingly alike. It turns out that the happiness of most people everywhere – in rich and poor countries, democratic and authoritarian – depends mainly on the same three broad personal concerns – first of all, their economic situation, and then, family life and health (Cantril, 1965).

When one thinks about it, this worldwide similarity in responses makes sense. Wherever they live, most people's lives are taken up chiefly with making a living and family and health issues. These are matters which people tend to think they can control themselves, at least to some degree, as opposed to broad structural concerns like type of government or socio-economic inequality. Detailed types of concern – say, the particular content of "economic situation" – sometimes differ among countries. Thus, in an agricultural society, it might be "owning a farm of one's own"; in an industrial country, "a job that offers good opportunity for advancement." But everywhere a person's economic situation in general, whatever the specifics, tops the list of what people say is important for their happiness, with family and health concerns next.

The similarity in the sources of happiness is evidenced by the uniformity of happiness relations from country to country to a wide variety of circumstances, such as age, income, education, health, partnership status, and employment status. For example, surveys of happiness almost invariably find that, on average, greater happiness is associated with higher income and having a partner, and that happiness is adversely affected by unemployment and poor health. For references that cover the broad set of influences on happiness see Clark (2018), Helliwell et al. (2012), and Layard (2005).

It is this similarity among people in the underlying determinants of happiness that makes it meaningful to average the individual responses, and to compare the changes in happiness over time and the differences among and within countries. This is not to say that happiness can easily be compared on a person-to-person basis. But when we study groups of people, individual differences frequently average out, and the result is dominated by the very large proportion of persons for whom the sources of happiness are essentially the same.

There is some disagreement, however. Three studies argue that happiness scores are not always comparable across people (Bertrand and Mullainathan, 2001; Bond and Lang, 2019; Schröder and Yitzhaki, 2017). Additional studies discuss how individuals may change their responses over time (Fabian, 2022; Prati and Senik, 2022), or have different cultural priorities, especially when contrasting Europe with Asian countries (Hitokoto and Uchida, 2015; Hornsey et al., 2018; Krys et al., 2019). However, it could be argued that these studies have led to an improvement in the measurement of happiness, showing the ideal conditions to measure and use happiness (Chen et al., 2022; Kaiser and Lepinteur, 2024; Kaiser and Vendrik, 2019). For instance, three papers use innovative survey instruments to adjust raw happiness responses to improve comparability across people (Angelini et al., 2014; Benjamin et al., 2023; Montgomery, 2022).

Although measurement can be improved, researchers and institutions have demonstrated that the existing happiness measures consistently reflect feelings of well-being, that is, they are *reliable* and *valid* in a psychometric sense. This property of happiness measures represents the third answer to whether they are meaningful. Reliability is displayed by showing respondents provide consistent answers across short periods of time. Demonstrating validity is accomplished by correlating happiness scores with metrics that we expect to be correlated with happiness according to theory. For instance, happiness scores are related to biometric data, such as from functional magnetic resonance imaging (commonly known as fMRI) scans. Greater happiness is associated with higher income and having a partner, as mentioned previously. Happiness scores also predict factors that we believe they should (Helliwell et al., 2012). For example, the response to a question related to life expectations in 1970 better predicted how long the respondent was going to live than their income level (O'Connor and Graham, 2019). For a complete discussion of the reliability and validity of happiness measures, see the OECD guidelines for measuring subjective well-being (Mahoney, 2023; OECD, 2013).

Presently the OECD is engaged in incorporating all of these perspectives in their guidelines on how to measure subjective well-being (Mahoney, 2023; OECD, 2013), and has thus far not recommended changing the types of questions that we use to measure happiness. While these issues are being resolved, the Happiness Revolution advances. Today, happiness is collected across the European Union by the official statistical offices of each member state.

1.3 Foundations of the Happiness Revolution

The main contributors to the Happiness Revolution are readily sketched. The first achievement of the social sciences was in laying the foundation for the Happiness Revolution by establishing widespread recognition that social ills like unemployment, poor health, and poverty are due, not to personal defects – the typical view in the past – but to circumstances beyond an individual's control. They require collective action to help those suffering from them. Policies to achieve this goal have chiefly taken two forms, economic and social.

Highlighting early *economic policy*, several national and international institutions were established throughout the twentieth century to promote maximum employment, control inflation, and increase economic stability. Although the institutions' creators did not have happiness in mind, as measured today, there was at least an intuitive understanding of the causes of happiness and misery. For instance, in the 1970s, Arthur Okun created the Misery Index as the sum of the unemployment and inflation rates. Today, we know Okun was not entirely wrong: perhaps not surprisingly, happiness is indeed lower in countries with high unemployment and / or high inflation (more to come on this later).

Among the first such institutions is the United States Federal Reserve. Established in 1913, today it is known in part for the "Dual Mandate" under which it operates to promote maximum employment and stable prices. This mandate was based in part on goals set forth in the Employment Act of 1946 stating: it is the policy and responsibility of the federal government "[. . .] to foster and promote free competitive enterprise and the *general welfare*, conditions under which there will be afforded useful employment, for those able, willing, and seeking work, and to promote maximum employment, production, and purchasing power (Steelman, 2011, p. 1, emphasis added)." It is not surprising that production was a priority of economic policy following World War II, but employment and purchasing power appear equally important here. (Controlling inflation is necessary to ensure stable prices and purchasing power.)

Among the first European institutions was the International Labour Organization (ILO), which was established in 1919 following World War I. It was created to improve workers' conditions, which were then seen as a source of social injustice that threatened lasting peace in Europe (ILO, 2024).

Internationally, the Bretton Woods Agreement was signed in 1944 to create an efficient foreign exchange system, and thereby facilitate global finance, international trade, and ultimately the economic integration of countries around the world. As part of this agreement, the International Monetary Fund (IMF) and World Bank were established. Such integration is seen as a means to promote economic welfare and reduce military conflict.[3]

On the *social policy* side are programs comprising what is often called the "social safety net." They include, but are not limited to, income support (unemployment insurance, social security, social assistance, and disability benefits), universal healthcare, infant and childcare, education (including early age schooling), maternity and paternity leave, elderly care, and old age pensions. These social policy initiatives, which are still evolving, are most fully realized in today's welfare state. According to the results of national surveys, the cradle-to-grave measures of the welfare state address the concerns most important for personal happiness of people throughout the world – employment and income security, a fulfilling family life, and good health (Cantril, 1965).

The evolution of social spending over the twentieth century illustrates how governments increased their emphasis on the social safety net over time. Social programs generally began in more developed countries and then spread throughout the world. Today, public social spending averages around 15 percent of GDP in Europe (excluding public education expenditures), but prior to 1900, only Spain and Great Britain reached spending levels of even one percent. Expenditures began to take off in the 1930s and 1940s, reaching five percent in several countries by 1950, and continuing to increase into today (OECD, 2021), reaching maximum levels of just over 30 percent of the economy.

Unfortunately, happiness data are not available to assess the early policy innovations. Limited happiness data exist prior to the 1980s, but we can point to numerous conditions that are believed to contribute to well-being: those that relate to the Industrial and Demographic Revolutions, including income and

[3] For example, the predecessor of the European Union, the European Economic Community, was established with this motivation in mind.

health, as well as data on education, income inequality, democracy, crime, and environmental conditions. Combining these indicators into one composite index suggests well-being increased nearly continuously in Europe from when the data began in 1820 onwards (van Zanden et al., 2014). This trend is suggestive that happiness would have improved over the twentieth century, but as discussed in the next section, happiness depends on more than objective conditions alone – it also depends on how one perceives those conditions.

Of course not all twentieth-century policy was intended to support happiness. It was believed by many that the actions of self-interested individuals would lead to the best societal outcomes – often referencing the "invisible hand" of Adam Smith – and that the best way to support individual action was through a decentralized market. Thus, in their view, a healthy market led to the best societal outcomes. This view, combined with statistical innovations in measuring national production – that is, gross domestic product (GDP), used as a proxy for market health – led to the goal of maximizing GDP alone. If the views were correct, then GDP growth would translate into improving happiness. However, for many, GDP became the ultimate goal over the course of the twentieth century and happiness was forgotten.

> The paradox is that those who built the system [of national accounts, which includes GDP] knew of its shortcomings and were cautious when using it. But as the general understanding of these indicators and their construction diminished, their use became more widespread and their limits were forgotten by most users. While GDP had been designed and used to measure market activity, increasingly it became a thermometer used for assessing the general health of societies. (Stiglitz et al., 2018, p. 19)

The above quote describes how GDP was never intended to be a policy target per se. In 1968, U.S. presidential candidate Robert Kennedy, famously said:

> The gross national product [GNP, similar to GDP] does not allow for the health of our children, the quality of their education or the joy of their play. It does not include the beauty of our poetry or the strength of our marriages, the intelligence of our public debate or the integrity of our public officials. It measures neither our wit nor our courage, neither our wisdom nor our learning, neither our compassion nor our devotion to our country, it measures everything in short, except that which makes life worthwhile. (Robert Kennedy 1968)

Since, two notable movements have contributed to reorienting decision-making back to well-being and happiness. In the 1970s, the Social Indicators Movement aimed to provide the noneconomic statistics necessary to monitor a more complete concept of well-being (Land et al., 2012; Sirgy et al., 2006). In the last twenty years, the Beyond GDP Movement has become influential. Perhaps the best-known example of this movement is the previously mentioned *Commission on the Measurement of Economic Performance and Social Progress*, which recommended measuring objective and subjective well-being. Success is suggested by the number of countries that have followed suit. Today, more than 70 percent of OECD countries have developed national frameworks to measure, monitor, and report well-being – frameworks that typically involved extensive public consultation to ascertain what the public cares about.

1.4 Does Happiness Increase with GDP and Life Expectancy? Changing References Levels

Improvements in GDP and life expectancy undoubtedly contributed to the foundations of the Happiness Revolution, yet the ongoing revolution is a bit more complicated. People are frequently surprised to learn that measures of happiness do not vary with trends over time in GDP and life expectancy. In the United States, for example, over the past seventy years, GDP per capita (adjusted for the changing level of prices) has more than tripled and life expectancy has increased by greater than ten years, but happiness has, if anything, declined slightly (Easterlin, 1974; O'Connor, 2017). In China between 1990 and 2015 GDP per capita and life expectancy grew phenomenally, but happiness at the end of the period was much the same as at the beginning (Easterlin et al., 2017). The disparate course of happiness compared with the other two markers indicates that the Happiness Revolution is "one-of-a-kind," distinct from the other two break-throughs in the human condition, and results from its own special circumstances.

But some may reasonably ask: how can people not be happier if their living conditions and life expectancy are vastly improved? The answer turns on recognizing that happiness is subjective and depends not only on observed living conditions, but on the internal scale by which people evaluate those conditions (Diener et al., 1985). This relationship was described some thirty years ago by psychologists Amos Tversky and Daniel Kahneman (Tversky and Kahneman, 1991). They found that people's feelings about a particular circumstance depend on an internal *reference level*, a benchmark against which they judge the situation. For example, is a man 5 feet, 9 inches, a *tall* man? The answer depends on one's reference level for height. In India, where the average height of men is 5 feet, 6 inches, he is likely to be judged as tall. But in the United States, where the average height of men is 5 feet, 10 inches, he would not be so regarded. In both countries, people are forming a reference level based on their observations of the people around them.

You likely know the goal of "keeping up with the Jones." We call this social comparison. Whether you feel like your income is a lot or a little depends on how it compares with others' incomes – those who earn more than others generally feel happier, while those who earn less are less happy, and this holds regardless of one's income in absolute terms, irrespective of others'. People also tend to compare upwards (Clark and d'Ambrosio, 2015; Clark and Senik, 2010) – meaning that people generally set their reference incomes above their own and compare with people who earn more than they do.

Social comparison undercuts the societal benefits of increasing income. When an individual's income increases, it increases relative to their reference level and their happiness increases, but at the same time, this increases the reference level for others. Consequently, one person is made better off while another one is made worse off and there is no increase in national happiness.[4] Thankfully, not everything is easily comparable. For example, people do not actually compare incomes; they tend to compare spending on what we call conspicuous consumption, such as vehicles and clothing. Whereas education, housing, healthcare, and savings are less conspicuous and therefore less subject to social comparison (Wu, 2020). This means it is possible for some improving circumstances to largely escape the negative effects of social comparison.

Similarly, how people perceive their living and health circumstances depends on a reference level governed by their personal experience. People living today have a reference level determined by the circumstances of today, but people living in the past had a reference level governed, not by today's conditions, but rather by the less favorable conditions that they experienced at that time. As conditions improve, people tend to habituate or adapt to those conditions and increase their reference levels (Easterlin, 2001). We call this process adaptation. As a result of adaptation, people today would evaluate the circumstances of the past less favorably than the people of the past would have – we have come to expect to earn more and live longer.

Ultimately, it is these differences in reference levels that explain why greater happiness does not necessarily accompany advances in living and health conditions. Increasing reference levels undercut the perceived benefits of improving conditions. It is for this reason – changing reference levels – that analyses of the drivers of happiness should generally utilize happiness changes that occur over time and not cross-sectional analyses that compare differences across people or countries at one point in time.

Changing reference levels does not necessarily mean happiness levels are doomed to stay constant over time. Happiness has doubtless moved inversely with famines and epidemics, and the Happiness Revolution saw the advent of

[4] Absolute income increases (irrespective of others) could still improve happiness, but they are also subject to adaptation, discussed next, and ultimately, the evidence shows national GDP growth does not have a lasting effect on happiness. More on this in Section 3.

policies specifically directed toward people's foremost concerns, which increases happiness. Section 2 demonstrates the substantial differences in happiness among regions around the world. There is no reason to suspect lower-scoring nations cannot achieve higher scores, and we do observe meaningful and lasting changes in happiness. For instance, African Americans in the United States experienced large increases in happiness since the 1970s (O'Connor, 2017), Japan's happiness notably increased over the twenty-year period from 1990 to 2010 (Sarracino et al., 2022), and as will be shown in Section 2, so did happiness in several European nations.

1.5 Outline

Our principal purpose here is to sketch quantitatively the course of the Happiness Revolution across the face of Europe since the latter part of the twentieth century – what has happened and why. In several European countries the Happiness Revolution started as much as a century earlier, but it is only since the 1980s that reliable and fairly comprehensive and comparable time-series measures of subjective well-being in Europe have become available.

In what follows we first identify in Section 2 Europe's ranking in the worldwide picture of happiness, the major differences in current levels of happiness among European countries, and the long-term trends in happiness in the principal regions of Europe since the late twentieth century. Section 3 looks at the principal factors behind the long-term trends. Section 4 focuses on happiness inequality among persons within individual countries, and its change over time. Section 5 discusses happiness differences among various demographic groups and how changes in population characteristics (e.g., aging) may have contributed to long-term changes in happiness. Section 6 considers the recent influences on happiness coming from the COVID-19 pandemic. Section 7 summarizes and presents some concluding observations.

2 Happiness Rankings and Trends

2.1 Europe's Happiness in World Perspective

Europe is the world's leader in happiness. The seven happiest countries in the world, out of more than 150 *recently* surveyed in the Gallup World Poll, are European, five of them Nordic. The top seven are, in order, Finland, Denmark, Switzerland, Norway, Iceland, Netherlands, and Sweden. Then come two non-European countries, New Zealand and Canada, with Austria weighing in at number ten. From year-to-year there is a modest shifting of places throughout the 150+ country array. The ranking presented here is based on an average of happiness values for four years, 2016–2019.

Table 1 Mean happiness of countries on specified continent, 2016–2019 (Scale 0–10)

	Number of countries	Mean happiness
Europe	37	6.18
North America	13	6.17
South America	10	5.93
Asia	38	5.33
Africa	46	4.40

Note: The happiness measure is the GWP Best Possible Life. Oceania is omitted because there are data for only two of fourteen countries there. Five countries with fewer than one million in population were also omitted.
Source: Author calculations, Gallup World Poll (Gallup, 2020).

When this study was undertaken, the most recent year for which data were available was 2019, prior to the COVID-19 pandemic. The analysis presented in this Element focuses on the roughly four decades from 1981 to 2019 when continuous data for Europe as a whole first became available. It concludes with an update for the pandemic years, 2020–2022.

If we compare the current happiness of continents by averaging the means for the countries on each continent, Europe, not surprisingly, is in the lead (Table 1). Europe's mean happiness, on a zero to 10 scale, is 6.18; the mean of the countries in Africa, the lowest-ranking continent, is 4.40. This may not seem like a very big difference but consider this. In Poland, which has a mean about the same as the European average, almost two persons out of three report happiness values ranging from 6 to 10. In Tunisia, which has a mean about the same as the African average, less than one in three – half the number for Poland – report a happiness value in that range. This contrast between Poland and Tunisia is indicative of the large happiness difference between Europeans and Africans.

The present Element focuses on countries of Europe with populations greater than one million, thirty-seven in all. They are classified into five regions, as shown subsequently in Table 2. The Gallup World Poll, one of the principal sources of data used throughout the Element, provides current data on all thirty-seven countries. The other principal source used here, the EVS, covers all but six of the thirty-seven, omitting in recent years: Ireland, Belgium, Portugal, Latvia, Moldova, and Ukraine.

The averages reported here give equal weight to each country whether small or large, as will be true throughout this Element. If, in computing the average, the value for each country were weighted by its population size, the average

Table 2 Countries of Europe classified by region and mean happiness, 2016–2019

	Western Bloc (6.94)			Eastern Bloc (5.61)	
Mean happiness [a]	**Northern Europe (7.57)**	**Western Europe (7.22)**	**Southern Europe (6.24)**	**Cental and Eastern Europe (6.01)**	**Eastern Europe (FSU) (5.75)**
7.50–7.99	Finland (7.77) Denmark (7.62) Norway (7.52)	Switzerland (7.53)			
7.00–7.49	Sweden (7.36)	Netherlands (7.47) Austria (7.23) Great Britain (7.08) Ireland (7.08) Germany (7.03)			
6.50–6.99		Belgium (6.89) France (6.62)		Czech Republic (6.85)	
6.00–6.49			Spain (6.38) Italy (6.28)	Slovenia (6.25) Slovak Republic (6.21) Poland (6.18) Romania (6.08)	Lithuania (6.13)

5.50–5.99		Portugal (5.79)	Hungary (5.86) Serbia (5.76)	Latvia (5.95) Estonia (5.93) Moldova (5.6) Russia (5.6)
			Bosnia and Herzegovina (5.54)	
5.00–5.49		Greece (5.45)	Croatia (5.48) North Macedonia (5.21) Bulgaria (5.04)	Belarus (5.45)
4.00–4.99			Albania (4.79)	Armenia (4.79) Georgia (4.61) Ukraine (4.43)

Note: Mean happiness of each country and region is shown in parentheses. The happiness measure is GWP Best Possible Life. FSU-Former Soviet Union.
[a] Czech Republic Data for 2016–18 only. Russia Data includes Jan.–Feb. 2020.
Source: Author calculations, Gallup World Poll (Gallup, 2020).

would be dominated by just a few large countries – Russia, Germany, UK, France, and Italy, which together account for more than half of the total population of Europe.

2.2 Current Happiness within Europe

Happiness tends to decline as one moves across the continent from Northern and Western Europe to Southern and Eastern Europe, with the lowest levels typically occurring in the countries of the Former Soviet Union (Table 2). Mean happiness by region ranges from a high of 7.57 in Northern Europe to a low of 5.75 in the former member states of the Soviet Union. Within each region there is variability among countries, and typically some overlap of the countries in a given region with those in adjacent regions. Aside from members of the Former Soviet Union, the countries of the Eastern Bloc are currently pretty much on a par with those of Southern Europe.

This regional ranking is shown also by markers of the Industrial and Demographic Revolutions – GDP per capita and life expectancy – but this should not be taken as indicative of causality running from the earlier revolutions to the Happiness Revolution. The sciences underlying each of the revolutions – natural, life, and social sciences – exhibit a similar geographical pattern of emergence and diffusion, from Western Europe outward, and it is this similar geographic ordering of places around the world that is responsible for the current similar geographical ranking of the three revolutions (Easterlin, 2012).

2.3 Long-Term Happiness Trends

Over the last four decades, the most sizeable happiness change by far has occurred in the Eastern Bloc as it transitioned from socialism to capitalism. Some may infer from this statement that what was happening was an increase in happiness in Eastern Europe as it moved to capitalism. In fact, the opposite was the case. In the early 1980s the Eastern Bloc, under socialism, was not far from par with the Western Bloc. Subsequently, during the transition to capitalism, happiness there plummeted, reaching a low around the turn of the century. Since then, happiness has tended to recover, though typically it is still somewhat short of its initial value (Figure 1).

Within the Western Bloc, there has been no change in the ranking of regions – it remains: Northern, Western, and Southern. In this Bloc, there was mild regional convergence toward the end of the last century, as the Northern Region slipped slightly due to marked declines in Sweden and Denmark, and the other two regions, gained, as sizeable increases occurred in France, Germany, Spain, and Italy.

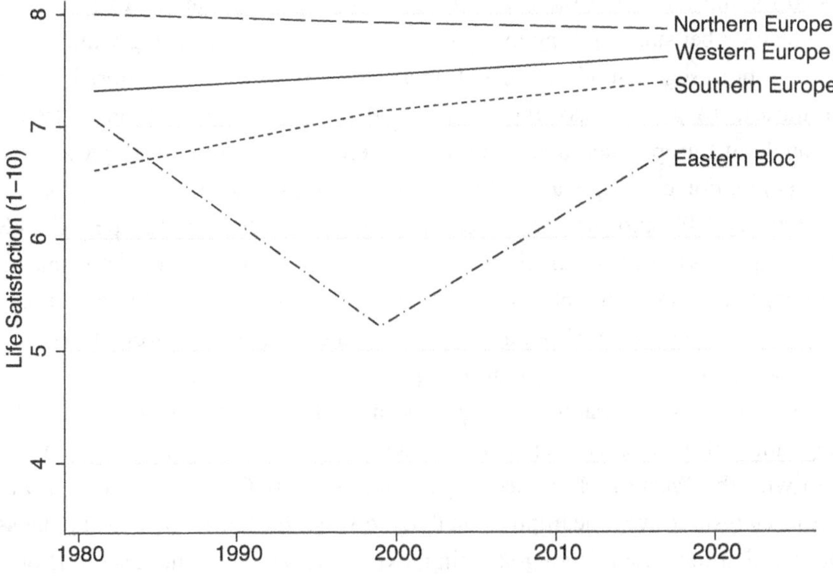

Figure 1 Happiness by region, ca. 1981–2018.

The happiness measure is EVS life satisfaction for three periods: 1981–1982, 1999–2000, and 2017–2018. Countries in each region are: Northern Europe – Norway, Sweden, Denmark, Finland; Western Europe – Great Britain, Netherlands, France, Germany; Southern Europe – Italy, Spain; and Eastern Bloc – Hungary, Russia.

Source: Author calculations, European Values Study, World Values Survey (EVS, 2015, 2020; Haerpfer et al., 2020; Inglehart et al., 2018).

These trend patterns are based on twelve Western and Eastern Bloc countries, the only ones for which there are data in all waves of the EVS. There have been five EVS surveys conducted about every nine years since 1981, but to bring out the longer-term movements, we have plotted in Figure 1 data for only three waves, 1981–1982, 1999–2000, and 2017–2018. Economic conditions in the initial and terminal waves, as judged by unemployment rates, were fairly similar overall, facilitating trend comparisons, but the regional picture would not have been much different if the start date were wave 2, 1990–1991.

An alternative data source, the Eurobarometer, covers a slightly longer period with much more detailed temporal coverage (typically semiannual), but it omits many Eastern Bloc countries, especially countries of the Former Soviet Union, and it also misses in the early years of the survey a number of Western Bloc countries as well, so long-term trends in Europe as a whole cannot be reliably determined. Moreover, the Eurobarometer happiness scale is only 1–4 versus

1–10 for the EVS, and the Eurobarometer only surveys natives of European Union member states, failing to register the status of the increasingly important foreign-born segment of the population, as much as 10 percent or more in some countries. To get a reasonably accurate idea of long-term happiness trends throughout Europe, therefore, the EVS is preferable, because of its geographic and population coverage, as well as its more extensive scale.

Between 1981 and 2018 among countries for which there are full-period EVS data, happiness increased in eight nations, declined in three, and did not change in one. On average, the change in happiness per decade for all twelve taken together is a positive 0.04 points on a 1–10 scale, with a range from a low of –0.24 points in Russia to a high of 0.25 points in Spain (Table 3).

Most published research on happiness in the Eastern Bloc starts around the beginning of the twenty-first century and reports a narrowing of the happiness gap with the Western Bloc (see, e.g., (Nikolova, 2016)). This is correct, but some analysts convey the impression that the West–East difference in happiness observed around 2000 is long-standing, extending back into the Eastern Bloc's socialist years. This inference is contradicted by the actual trends depicted in Figure 1, which started two decades prior to the turn of the century. According to the figure, happiness differences between Eastern and Western Bloc countries were much smaller in the early 1980s than at the turn of the century. Over the roughly four-decade period as a whole, East–West differences first widened noticeably and then narrowed.

In 1981–82, the two Eastern Bloc countries with happiness data were more or less on a par with the countries of Southern and Western Europe. (See the matrix of happiness by region, Table 4.) By the turn of the century, however, happiness in these two as well as the much larger number of Eastern Bloc countries included in the turn-of-the-century survey was typically below that in Southern Europe (Table 5). Then, by the end of the period most Eastern Bloc countries other than those in the Former Soviet Union climbed back to a substantial overlap with Southern Europe, narrowing the happiness gap (Table 2). It is the post-2000 segment of the longer-term trend that is most often reported in the literature. By starting with the happiness picture around 2000, a misleading impression is conveyed of the relative position of the Eastern Bloc earlier in the twentieth century.

The initially fairly high position of the Eastern Bloc when still socialist, may come as a surprise. True, the 1981–1982 happiness value for the Eastern Bloc is an average for only two countries, Hungary and Russia. Moreover, the value for Russia is based on one geographic division, Tambov, though there is evidence that Tambov is fairly representative of Russia as a whole. For example, in a

Table 3 Change in happiness between EVS Waves 1 and 5, by country and region

	(1)	(2)	(3)
Region and country	**Period**	**Total change**	**Average change per decade**
	(years)	**(scale 1–10)**	**(scale 1–10)**
All		0.13	0.04
Western Bloc		0.22	0.06
Northern		−0.14	−0.04
Norway	1982–2018	0.12	0.03
Sweden	1982–2017	−0.37	−0.11
Finland	1981–2017	−0.01	0.00
Denmark	1981–2017	−0.31	−0.09
Western		0.29	0.08
Great Britain	1981–2018	0.05	0.01
France	1981–2018	0.60	0.16
Netherlands	1981–2017	0.13	0.04
Germany	1981–2017	0.39	0.11
Southern		0.77	0.21
Spain	1981–2017	0.89	0.25
Italy	1981–2018	0.66	0.18
Eastern Bloc		−0.30	−0.09
Central and Eastern		0.22	0.06
Hungary	1982–2018	0.22	0.06
Former Soviet Union		−0.83	−0.24
Russia	1982–2017	−0.83	−0.24

Note: The measure of happiness is EVS Life Satisfaction. Russia figures for 1982 are for Tambov Oblast. Happiness differences are statistically significant at five percent or better, except Norway, Finland, and Great Britain – the countries with the three smallest changes in happiness.

Source: Author calculations, EVS/WVS (EVS, 2015, 2020; Haerpfer et al., 2020; Inglehart et al., 2018).

comparison of happiness in 1995, Tambov's mean happiness was 4.23; Russia's, 4.45 (Easterlin, 2010, pp. 104–105; Inglehart and Klingemann, 2000, p. 175).

There are two pieces of empirical evidence based on a broader range of Eastern Bloc countries that provide additional support for the inference of a noticeable decline in happiness during the transition of the Eastern Bloc to capitalism. Every single one of the twenty-one Eastern Bloc countries experienced a collapse in GDP at the start of the transition to capitalism. Usually, this decline in total output

Table 4 Twelve countries of Europe with full period EVS data classified by region and mean happiness, 1981–82

		Western Bloc (7.45)		Eastern Bloc (7.06)	
Mean happiness	**Northern Europe (8)**	**Western Europe (7.32)**	**Southern Europe (6.61)**	**Central and Eastern Europe (6.93)**	**Eastern Europe (FSU) (7.2)**
8.00–8.49	Denmark (8.21)				
7.50–7.99	Finland (7.91) Norway (7.89)	Netherlands (7.7)			
7.00–7.49		Germany (7.25)			Russia (7.2)
6.50–6.99		France (6.66)	Italy (6.62) Spain (6.6)	Hungary (6.93)	

Note: Mean happiness of each country and region is shown in parentheses. The happiness measure is EVS Life Satisfaction.
Source: Author calculations, EVS (EVS, 2015, 2020) Russia / Tambov 1982 (Easterlin, 2010, pp. 104–105).

Table 5 Countries of Europe with EVS data classified by region and mean happiness, 1999–2000

	Western Bloc (7.57)			Eastern Bloc (5.47)	
Mean[a] happiness	**Northern Europe (7.86)**	**Western Europe (7.71)**	**Southern Europe (6.98)**	**Central and Eastern Europe (5.92)**	**Eastern Europe (FSU) (4.88)**
8.00–8.49	Denmark (8.24)	Ireland (8.17) Switzerland (8.14) Austria (8.02)			
7.50–7.99	Finland (7.87) Norway (7.66) Sweden (7. 65)	Netherlands (7.88) Germany (7.61)			
7.00–7.49		Belgium (7.56) Great Britain (7.4)	Italy (7.17) Spain (7.09)	Slovenia (7.23) Czech Republic (7.06)	
6.50–6.99		France (6.93)	Portugal (6.98) Greece (6.67)		
6.00–6.49				Croatia (6.46) Poland (6.37) Slovak Republic (6.03)	
5.50–5.99				Hungary (5.69) Serbia (5.62) Bosnia and Herzegovina (5.61)	Estonia (5.9)
5.00–5.49				North Macedonia (5.41) Bulgaria (5.34)	Latvia (5.27)

Table 5 (cont.)

	Western Bloc (7.57)			Eastern Bloc (5.47)	
Mean[a] happiness	**Northern Europe (7.86)**	**Western Europe (7.71)**	**Southern Europe (6.98)**	**Central and Eastern Europe (5.92)**	**Eastern Europe (FSU) (4.88)**
				Romania (5.23) Lithuania (5.09)	
4.00–4.99				Albania (4.97)	Belarus (4.81) Russia (4.74) Georgia (4.68) Moldova (4.57) Ukraine (4.56) Armenia (4.32)

Note: Mean happiness of each country and region is shown in parentheses. The happiness measure is EVS Life Satisfaction.

[a]EVS data are from 1999 to 2000. WVS data were necessary when EVS Wave 3 was not conducted in a country, including Albania (avg. 1998, 2002), Armenia (1997), Bosnia and Herzegovina (avg. 1998, 2001), Georgia (1996), North Macedonia (avg. 1998, 2001), Moldova (2002), Montenegro (2001), Serbia (2001), and Switzerland (1996),

Source: Author calculations, EVS/WVS (EVS, 2015, 2020; Haerpfer et al., 2020; Inglehart et al., 2018).

is one of substantial magnitude (Figures 2 and 3). Although only nine of the twenty-one countries have happiness data covering most or all of the period of GDP contraction, in every single one of these nine countries there is a decline in happiness corresponding to that in GDP (Easterlin, 2010, pp. 104–105, 109–110).

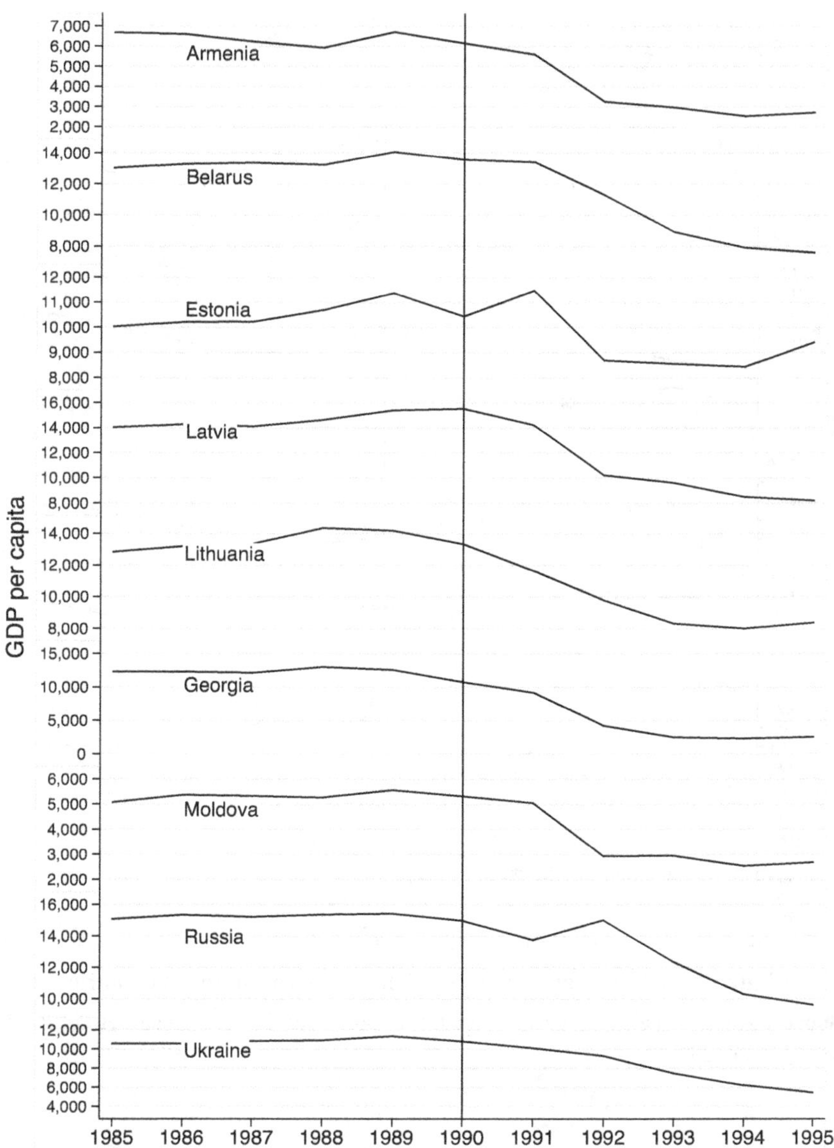

Figure 2 GDP Per capita in former Soviet Union countries.

Source: Authors' calculations data are from (Bolt et al. 2018; Feenstra et al., 2015; World Bank, 2020).

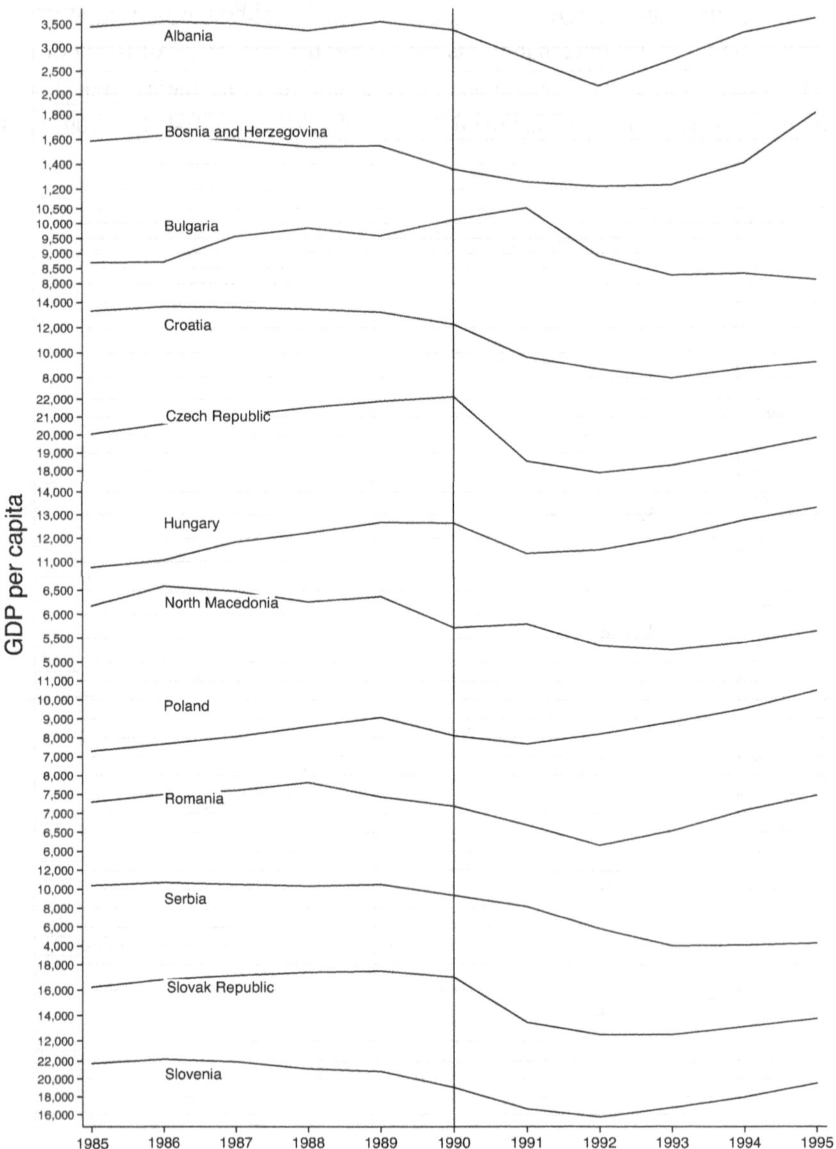

Figure 3 GDP per capita in Central and Eastern European countries.

Source: Authors' calculations data are from (Bolt et al. 2018; Feenstra et al., 2015; World Bank, 2020).

Hence, it is reasonable to infer that during the transition to capitalism happiness declined along with GDP from initially higher values in all of the twenty-one countries of the Eastern Bloc, and the declines are not observed in some countries simply because of the lack of pre-transition happiness data.

A comparison of the magnitude of the happiness changes after 2000 in Eastern versus Western Bloc countries also points to a happiness decline in the Eastern Bloc before the turn of the century. Since the beginning of the twenty-first century there is an increase in happiness in every country of the Eastern Bloc and by a substantial amount – the mean change is 1.50 on a 1–10 scale.[5] In contrast, among thirteen countries of the Western Bloc (with EVS data), six experienced decreasing happiness, and the mean change for all thirteen is only 0.20 (irrespective of direction, positive or negative). The sizeable difference in the magnitude of the happiness changes between the two Blocs after 2000 is consistent with the view that the Eastern Bloc was recovering from a previous substantial happiness decline.

Since 2000, a period when we have fairly comprehensive country coverage, there is substantial stability in the ordering of the countries within both the Western and Eastern Blocs (Tables 2 and 4). Usually, the changes in rank order that occur amount to only a few places, up or down. Sizeable improvements in rank order by as much as five or more places are limited to Finland in the West and Lithuania, Moldova, Romania, and Russia in the East. Declines in rank order of five places or more occur in Ireland in the West and Bulgaria, Croatia, and North Macedonia in the East.

3 Long-Term Trends in Happiness: Driving Forces[6]

The long-term trends in happiness described earlier are principally the result of government welfare policies and changing income inequality.[6] We have noted that when it comes to happiness most people are chiefly concerned about their economic situation, family circumstances, and health. In the period studied here, some countries were expanding government programs directed toward these concerns; others were retreating from such policies, and in some, welfare policies declined and then partially or wholly recovered. Peoples' happiness responded positively to expansion, negatively to retreat. At the same time, income inequality negatively affected happiness – the greater the increase in inequality, the larger the decrease in happiness. Other oft-mentioned factors, such as economic growth, inflation, life expectancy, or social capital, do not robustly explain the happiness trends, as evidenced by the statistical analysis that follows. Similarly, joining the EU did not have a systematically positive or negative effect on happiness.

[5] This is visible using EVS data, not in comparing Tables 2 with Table 5. That is because Table 2 displays happiness from the Gallup World Poll, which uses a 0–10 scale, while the EVS uses a 1–10 scale.

[6] This section is based in part on previous work conducted by the authors (Easterlin and O'Connor, 2022b).

3.1 Explanatory Variables

In the statistical analysis that follows, we consider eight possible determinants of happiness: two measures of social policy, the generosity of social welfare programs and government spending on such programs; three measures of economic policy, economic growth, represented by real GDP per capita, the unemployment rate, and inflation; and three additional variables, income inequality, which reflects both social and economic policy (among other influences), life expectancy, and the quality of social relations, approximated by responses to a query on "trust in others."

The generosity measure covers three types of social welfare programs – unemployment insurance, pensions, and sickness insurance. This measure, developed by Lyle Scruggs and his collaborators (Scruggs, 2022, 2006) is derived from detailed and painstaking study of the legislation and regulations relating to each of these social insurance programs in each country. Generosity increases with program characteristics such as a higher benefit replacement rate (the ratio of the after-tax cash benefit to after-tax wages), longer duration of benefit, and greater ease of qualification. Based on such characteristics a generosity index is developed for each of the three programs. These three indexes are then combined to obtain a total generosity index, the measure used here. (For details of index construction see Scruggs and Ramalho Tafoya, 2022).

The generosity index is a measure that depends upon benefit *policies*, which guarantee the *rights* to benefits; it is not an expenditure measure. Changes in the index can affect the happiness of a person whether or not that person actually collects benefits. Most people, for example, are not collecting sickness benefits, but knowing that such rights exist if they become sick removes a source of anxiety and makes them happier. Similarly, persons with jobs are happier because of the availability of unemployment insurance should they lose their jobs (Carr and Chung, 2014). A limitation of the Scruggs generosity index is that it does not cover all types of social welfare programs.

The second measure of government welfare programs is government spending on social protection. Although useful for some purposes, spending measures can be misleading with regard to happiness effects. Spending can increase without any change in policy or effect on happiness simply because of an increase in the number of persons collecting the benefit (e.g., more unemployed, or more retirees). We try to control for such influences by using a social spending measure that is adjusted to remove the influence of the unemployment rate and percentage of people over age 65.

Income inequality is a result of both economic and social policy, but unlike inflation and unemployment, it has not always been a concern nor was it foundational to the Happiness Revolution. It likely became more important over time. Hirschman (1973) argues that income inequality is tolerated to a greater degree during the early stages of economic development – when the Happiness Revolution began – but that this tolerance fades over time as people expect inequality to narrow in the later stages of development. And indeed, income inequality has a different relationship with happiness depending on the characteristics of the country; for instance, it tends to be more negatively perceived in Western Europe and positively perceived in Eastern Europe (Delhey and Dragolov, 2014). Income inequality may not have been foundational to the Happiness Revolution, but nonetheless, it may have had a significant influence on happiness and can itself be influenced by social policy. Greater income equality is a byproduct of social policy – the social safety net is typically paid for with progressive tax policies and provides services that particularly benefit lower-income groups.

Income inequality can affect happiness through three distinct pathways: first, through income comparisons or relative income (Clark and d'Ambrosio, 2015). When a rise in income inequality occurs, there is unequal income growth and those whose incomes grew at a slower rate feel worse off compared to those whose incomes grew at a faster rate; this occurs through the process of social comparison mentioned in Section 1. Second, rising incomes may signal your income will also rise soon, in which case, greater income inequality may be perceived positively – in a phenomenon referred to as the tunnel effect (Hirschman, 1973; Senik, 2004). The third pathway is through societal influences and individuals' preferences over society. People tend to perceive high income inequality as unfair and trust less in highly unequal conditions (Oishi et al., 2011). But this experience may vary by country, for instance, Europeans tend to perceive income inequality worse than Americans (Alesina et al., 2004).

Concerning the other variables, greater GDP and life expectancy are thought to be good things, as discussed in Section 1, while increases in unemployment and inflation are assumed to be bad, as in the Misery Index (mentioned in Section 1) and based on previous results in the scientific literature (Blanchflower et al., 2014; Di Tella et al., 2003, 2001). Trust in others is a form of social capital, which is often held up as one of the strongest predictors of happiness – happier people are more trusting, and more trusting people are happier (Guven, 2011; Sarracino and Slater, 2024).

The explanatory variables are measured in the usual way: real GDP per capita (adjusted for inflation), unemployment (unemployed as a percentage of the labor force), and inflation (percentage change in consumer prices). Income inequality is measured using the Gini coefficient on after tax income – a greater Gini coefficient reflects greater income inequality. Life expectancy is short for life expectancy at birth, the most commonly used measure. Each variable is obtained from publicly available data sources, typically prepared by national statistical offices and then shared by international organizations like the World Bank. Trust in others is the proportion of respondents that replied most people can be trusted from the survey question, "Generally speaking would you say that most people can be trusted or that you can't be too careful in dealing with people?" obtained from the same EVS surveys that are used for happiness. See the table notes for details.

Our statistical analysis is fairly simple. For countries with the necessary data, we compute the change between the early 1980s and late 2010s in happiness and each of the explanatory variables described earlier. We then explore via regression analysis which of the explanatory variables are linked to the change in happiness during that period. In addition to this time-series analysis that covers the full-period change, we use a similar estimation technique to test the robustness of the relations; specifically, a set of fixed-effects regressions on the pooled observations from all five EVS surveys. We discuss the fixed effects approach in more detail at the end of this section in the appendix. The basic data are presented in Table 9 (in Section 3.4). Because of data constraints, the quantitative analysis is limited to Western Bloc countries, but we show qualitatively that the experience of Eastern Bloc countries fits the picture based on the Western Bloc. We also demonstrate that point-of-time (cross-section) analysis gives a misleading impression of causal relations and suggest why this is so.

3.2 Statistical Results

The trend in life satisfaction is chiefly related to two variables, the generosity of a country's welfare programs and the change in income inequality – increased generosity goes with greater happiness, while increased inequality is associated with lower happiness. In bivariate regressions of the full-period change in happiness on each of the possible explanatory variables, four statistically significant relations are found (presented in Table 6), but only two are robust. The first is between program generosity and happiness. This is readily observable in the raw data too. Spain and Italy have the largest increases in both life satisfaction and program generosity, while Denmark and Sweden have the largest decreases in both (see Table 9 in Section 3.4). The second robust relation is between income inequality and happiness, which is also observable in data. France is the only country that experienced declining income inequality and it had one of the largest increases in happiness. Sweden and Finland, on the other hand, had the largest increases in income inequality and were among the only three countries that experienced declining happiness. Inflation and life expectancy are also statistically significantly related to happiness in the time-series analysis (Table 6), but the relations are not robust to alternative statistical estimation techniques.

The robustness (fixed effects) analysis confirms program generosity and income inequality are robust predictors of the changes in happiness. They are the only significant variables, though at a lower significance level, $p < 0.10$ and $p < 0.05$, respectively; inflation and life expectancy lose statistical significance altogether (see Table 10 in Section 3.4). This conclusion, that greater generosity of welfare state programs is related to greater happiness over time, is also supported by the existing evidence (Di Tella et al., 2003; Easterlin, 2013; Sarracino et al., 2022), including some studies that plausibly establish a causal impact of welfare-state programs on happiness (De Grip et al., 2012; Gregg et al., 2009; Morgan and O'Connor, 2022). Inequality has also been shown to be negatively related to happiness over time in Europe (Alesina et al., 2004; Ebert and Welsch, 2009; Verme, 2011).

Thus the empirical evidence supports the Happiness Revolution and social policy as more important than economic policy. Expanding the social safety net is associated with increasing happiness. However, to accurately capture this relationship one needs to use program generosity. The amount of spending on social welfare is not significantly related to happiness (Table 6), even after adjusting for the confounders: unemployment and the size of the old-age population. Economic policy may have contributed in recent years through reduced inflation – each country experienced a decline in inflation over the period (Table 9), and decreasing inflation is associated with increasing happiness (Table 6), though not robustly, as mentioned. On the other hand, unemployment both increased and decreased over the period across countries, and is not statistically related to the change in happiness.

Greater changes in GDP per capita were also not related to greater changes in happiness. If the Industrial Revolution were responsible for the Happiness Revolution, one would have expected them to be related. But the evidence in Tables 6 and 10 indicates that the changes in GDP per capita have no significant impact, that is, that happiness is not affected by an increase in GDP per capita in a lasting way. This finding fits within a long-standing set of research surrounding what has become known as the Easterlin Paradox (Easterlin, 1974). The current finding confirms the original finding that economic growth does not contribute to happiness in the long run and is supported by recent work (Easterlin, 2017; Easterlin and O'Connor, 2022a). Likewise, the change in life expectancy is not robustly associated with the change in happiness (see Table 10), indicating that the Demographic Revolution also did not lead to the Happiness Revolution.

Table 6 Statistics for bivariate regression of change in happiness between EVS Waves 1 and 5 on change in specified explanatory variable

	(1)	(2)	(3)	(4)	(5)	(6)	(7)	(8)
Generosity	0.051** (0.046)							
Soc. Exp.		0.047 (0.186)						
GDPpc			0.294 (0.694)					
Unemployment				0.027 (0.466)				
Inflation					−0.056* (0.099)			
Income inequality						−0.124*** (0.005)		
Life expectancy							0.280** (0.012)	
Trust								−2.167 (0.104)

Constant	0.217*	0.163	−0.451	0.214	−0.325	0.618**	−1.855**	0.461*
	(0.070)	(0.245)	(0.791)	(0.148)	(0.345)	(0.011)	(0.024)	(0.072)
Observations	10	10	10	10	10	10	10	10
R-squared	0.445	0.127	0.030	0.057	0.233	0.431	0.474	0.221
Adj. *R*-squared	0.375	0.018	−0.091	−0.061	0.137	0.360	0.408	0.123

Note: Regression of the variable changes from 1981–1982 to 2017–2018, except social expenditures, which uses the period from 1985 to 2017–2018, and GDPpc, which uses the ratio of end of period divided by beginning of period values.

Sources: See the table notes for Table 9.

p-values in parentheses: * $p < 0.10$ ** $p < 0.05$ *** $p < 0.01$.

Social capital, as measured by trust, surprisingly does not explain the trends in happiness. The previous evidence indicates that greater social capital is associated with greater happiness (Helliwell, 2003; Helliwell et al., 2012), however much of this evidence is cross-sectional (Sarracino and Slater, 2024) and it is difficult to know if an increase in social capital causes an increase in happiness, happiness causes social capital, or if indeed a third variable is ultimately responsible for the movements in both. The limited number of time-series analyses also show happiness and social capital move together in the same direction (Bartolini and Bilancini, 2010; Bartolini and Sarracino, 2014), though they are based on somewhat different periods and countries. Ultimately, the insignificant relationship that we find does not disprove the previous studies, it simply means that the relation is not precise enough to be reliably estimated in our sample and, as is common, more research is necessary.

Although the quantitative data are largely limited to the Western Bloc, qualitative assessment suggests welfare state programs were likewise important for happiness in the Eastern Bloc. Under socialism, there had been what is sometimes called a "socialist greenhouse" (Sobotka, 2002, chap. 4). Jobs were assured, and most women and men of working age were in the labor force. Unemployment was virtually nonexistent. Employers provided childcare and financed comprehensive healthcare. With the transition to free markets, the guaranteed jobs that existed under socialism vanished; so did the perks of employment such as healthcare and childcare, and happiness plummeted.

Adaptation to the deteriorating social safety net differed between the countries of the Former Soviet Union and Eastern and Central Europe. Eastern and Central European economies struggled to preserve substantial elements of the safety net, while FSU governments, except for the Baltic states, did comparatively little (World Bank, 2002). The result was a disparate course of happiness in the two regions. In Eastern and Central Europe and the Balkan states happiness slowly recovered from the demise of the socialist greenhouse; in most FSU countries, it cratered.

In the two Eastern Bloc countries for which there are data, the full-period change in happiness demonstrates the foregoing pattern – happiness in Hungary increases by 0.22 points between the early 1980s and the present, while that in Russia declines by 0.83 points (Table 3). In the Eastern Bloc, as in the Western Bloc, the course of happiness conforms to that of the generosity of social welfare programs.

The previous results (in Table 6) pertain to the trends of happiness, corresponding to how happiness changes over time. Much of the results in the scientific literature and popular press focus instead on point-of-time (cross-section) analysis, because it only requires data from one point in time. However, point-of-time analysis gives a misleading impression of the determinants of happiness trends. We demonstrate this feature in bivariate cross-section regressions based on all countries for which the requisite data exist. Five of the eight determinants are statistically significant (Table 7), including generosity and income inequality, but also GDP per capita, unemployment, and trust.

The cross-section result points to GDP per capita, unemployment, and trust as prime movers of happiness (Table 7), but the time-series relations clearly challenge this conclusion (Tables 6 and 10). In the case of GDP per capita, the well-known cross-section relation is an artifact of the point-of-time method. As has been noted, GDP per capita is a marker of the Industrial Revolution; while measures of subjective well-being like happiness are markers of the Happiness Revolution. The two Revolutions stem, at bottom, from different advances in science – natural sciences in the case of the Industrial Revolution; social sciences, for the Happiness Revolution. Both revolutions, however, share in common a very similar geographic pattern of emergence and diffusion – starting in Northern and Western Europe, progressing to Southern Europe, then to Eastern Europe, and finally, the countries of the Former Soviet Union. Hence, the same set of countries is high on markers of both revolutions, while another set of countries is low on both makers, and in statistical analysis, a significant positive correlation between GDP per capita and happiness results. This significant cross-section correlation, however, is not due to a causal connection, but to the similar patterns of geographic diffusion. Time-series analysis is required to identify the actual factor(s) at work.

3.3 Impact of the European Union?

An important further question is whether joining the EU had any systematic effect on happiness. A thorough examination of this question could amount to a book in itself. The answer may differ across country and time as the EU broadened from six to twenty-eight countries and deepened to unify markets, legal standards, currencies, and increased opportunities to migrate. Each country started from different circumstances and needed to adjust to varying degrees before they could join (excluding the six founders).

To get a quick impression, we compared the trends in happiness between countries that joined the EU, were early EU members, and those that have not joined the EU. We have happiness data for fifteen countries from before and

Table 7 Statistics for bivariate regressions of happiness on specified explanatory variable, EVS Wave 5

	(1)	(2)	(3)	(4)	(5)	(6)	(7)	(8)
Generosity	0.062*							
	(0.076)							
Soc. Exp.		0.058						
		(0.303)						
ln(GDPpc)			1.968***					
			(0.000)					
Unemployment				−0.075***				
				(0.009)				
Inflation					0.103			
					(0.650)			
Income inequality						−0.108**		
						(0.028)		
Life expectancy							0.056	
							(0.736)	
Trust								2.132***
								(0.003)

Constant	5.456***	7 198***	−13.500***	8.203***	7.433***	10.765***	3.029	6.564***
	(0.001)	(0.000)	(0.004)	(0.000)	(0.000)	(0.000)	(0.823)	(0.000)
Observations	13	13	13	13	13	13	13	13
R-squared	0.455	0.153	0.825	0.694	0.017	0.324	0.011	0.741
Adj. *R*-squared	0.405	0.076	0.809	0.666	−0.072	0.263	−0.079	0.718

Note: variables are in levels, not changes. Ln(GDPpc) is the natural log of GDP per capita – as is standard in the scientific literature.

Source: see the notes in Table 9.

p-values in parentheses * $p < 0.10$ ** $p < 0.05$ *** $p < 0.01$.

after they joined the EU from the EVS. Of these, the majority, eleven were from the Eastern Bloc. The other twenty-two countries had a stable status, of which ten joined before we had happiness data, and the remaining twelve never joined (two in the Western Bloc and ten in the Eastern). Table 8 shows the country groups. We use the longest data series available for each country in the Western Bloc. In the Eastern Bloc, we restrict the data to the period starting after 1995, when more countries have an initial measurement of happiness. Eastern Bloc countries that joined the EU typically have earlier happiness measurements than the Eastern Bloc countries that did not join, which would have limited their comparability.

The associations are mixed. Happiness generally increased in the countries that joined the EU (Table 8, column 3), but in the Eastern Bloc, happiness increased at a faster rate in the non-EU (column 7). Perhaps the EU-joining countries from the Eastern Bloc would have experienced even greater increases in happiness if they had not joined. On the other hand, in the Western Bloc, happiness increased at about the same rate in each country group, new members (column 3), older members (column 5), and those who have not joined (column 7). Additional regression analysis (unreported) yields a null result – joining the EU is not statistically related to changes in happiness.

3.4 Appendix

Table 9 presents the basic data for the statistical analysis in Table 6.

Table 10 presents the results of the fixed effects analysis used to test the robustness of the results in Table 6. As mentioned earlier, only program generosity and income inequality are statistically significant. The fixed effects relations are interpreted similarly to the time-series associations. Fixed effects regressions include a dummy variable for each country and yield relations related to within-country changes in the variables over time, as opposed to differences in variables between countries. The main difference between the time-series and fixed-effects estimation techniques is the period of change and number of observations. The time-series relations apply to changes over approximately thirty-six years, while the fixed-effects relations apply to the periods between observations, approximately nine years. The total number of observations in the fixed effect regressions is forty-nine (Norway was not surveyed in EVS wave 3).

4 Happiness Differences and Inequality

The previous section was based on the average of happiness responses in each country. But some people are, of course, above average, and others, below. This section focuses on how happiness typically differs among persons within a

Table 8 Influence of the EU: Changes in EU status and happiness, thirty-seven countries, EVS

	(1)	(2)	(3)	(4)	(5)	(6)	(7)
		Joined EU		Early EU		Non-EU	
Region	**Period**	**# of countries**	**Happiness change/year**	**# of countries**	**Happiness change / year**	**# of countries**	**Happiness change/year**
Europe	1992–2016	15	0.05	10	0.00	12	0.10
Western Bloc	1984–2016	4	0.00	10	0.00	2	0.00
Northern	1982–2017	2	−0.01	1	−0.01	1	0.00
Western	1983–2015	1	0.00	6	0.01	1	−0.01
Southern	1988–2015	1	0.02	3	−0.01	0	
Eastern Bloc	1998–2016	11	0.07	0		10	0.12
Central and Eastern	1999–2018	8	0.06	0		4	0.09
Former Soviet Union	1998–2015	3	0.09	0		6	0.13

Note: Happiness data for the Western Bloc uses the longest series available by country. For the Eastern Bloc, we restricted data to the period following 1995, which harmonized the initial data point across countries.

Source: Author calculations, EVS/WVS (EVS, 2015, 2020; Haerpfer et al., 2020; Inglehart et al., 2018).

Table 9 Change in specified regression variable between Waves 1 and 5, countries ranked by size of change in life satisfaction

Country	Life satisfaction (scale)	Generosity index (0–100)	Social expenditures % of GDP	GDP_2/GDP_1	Unemployment %	Inflation %	Income inequality (0–100)	Life expectancy years	Trust (0–1)
Spain	0.89	3.62	1.85	2.75	3.05	−12.59	1.00	7.75	0.09
Italy	0.66	5.29	2.44	2.03	2.33	−16.83	3.00	8.99	0.02
France	0.60	2.41	4.23	1.89	1.48	−11.46	−0.10	8.42	0.04
Germany	0.39	−1.23	−0.58	2.50	−2.70	−4.83	4.10	8.04	0.14
Netherlands	0.13	−2.21	−4.34	2.17	−3.08	−5.36	3.40	5.83	0.21
Norway	0.12	3.37	4.46	2.42	2.10	−8.58	1.20	6.75	0.16
Great Britain	0.05	−1.89	2.33	2.21	−6.40	−9.58	4.70	7.23	−0.02
Finland	−0.01	7.26	3.58	2.16	3.60	−10.55	5.00	7.89	0.11
Denmark	−0.31	−7.59	1.46	2.26	−3.37	−10.62	2.80	6.87	0.28
Sweden	−0.37	−9.34	−4.08	2.24	3.58	−6.79	7.30	6.08	0.11
Average	0.22	−0.03	1.13	2.26	0.06	−9.72	3.24	7.39	0.11
Standard Dev.	0.41	5.43	3.17	0.24	3.59	3.59	2.19	1.02	0.09

Note: Changes in social expenditures are over the period 1985 to 2017–2018. GDP_2/GDP_1 represents the ratio of GDP per capita at the end of the period to the GDP per capita at the beginning of the period.

Source: *Life Satisfaction* and *Trust* are from EVS Surveys (EVS, 2015, 2020; Haerpfer et al., 2020; Inglehart et al., 2018). Trust is the proportion of respondents that replied most people can be trusted from question "Generally speaking would you say that most people can be trusted or that you can't be too careful in dealing with people?" *Generosity Index* (0–100) is from (Scruggs, 2022). IMF *social protection expenditures* (as a percentage of GDP) (IMF, 2020) was extended using ILO (ILO, 2014), OECD (OECD, 2018, and other IMF series (expenditures of the central government including social security funds). The expenditure series has also been adjusted to exclude the influence of changes in the unemployment rate and per cent of elderly population. *GDP per capita* is from the World Development Indicators (WDI) (World Bank, 2020) and then extended forward and backward as needed using real GDP per capita growth rates from Maddison (Bolt et al., 2018) and the Penn World Tables (Feenstra et al., 2015). *Unemployment, inflation* (using CPI), and *Life expectancy* (at birth) are also from the World Development Indicators (World Bank, 2020). The unemployment series is based on figures from national statistical offices and then extended forward and backward using International Labor Organization estimates – both from WDI. *Income inequality* (disposable income) is from the Standardized World Income Inequality Database (Solt, 2020).

Table 10 Statistics for fixed effects regressions of happiness on specified explanatory variables, EVS Waves 1 through 5

	(1)	(2)	(3)	(4)	(5)	(6)	(7)	(8)
Generosity	0.033* (0.072)							
Soc. Exp.		0.038 (0.133)						
ln(GDPpc)			0.859 (0.158)					
Unemployment				−0.010 (0.578)				
Inflation					−0.005 (0.797)			
Income inequality						−0.071** (0.010)		
Life expect.							0.107 (0.144)	
Trust								0.221 (0.754)

Constant	6.431***	7.271***	−1.363	7.659***	7.579***	9.538***	−0.800	7.469***
	(0.000)	(0.000)	(0.820)	(0.000)	(0.000)	(0.000)	(0.883)	(0.000)
Observations	49	49	49	49	49	49	49	49
R-squared	0.309	0.248	0.227	0.164	0.155	0.346	0.217	0.156

Note: Regressions of the full sample from 1981 to 2018; includes fixed effects by country (i.e., country dummies) and wave dummies. Variable values are in levels. Ln(GDPpc) is the natural log of GDP per capita – as is standard in the scientific literature.

Source: see the notes in Table 9.

p-values in parentheses (clustered by country) * $p < 0.10$ ** $p < 0.05$ *** $p < 0.01$.

country – in other words, how happiness is distributed within countries. More people at the lower and higher ends of the happiness scale represent more dispersion in the happiness distribution and greater happiness inequality. Not surprisingly, overall happiness tends to be greater when happiness inequality is less.

4.1 How Respondents Are Distributed on the Happiness Scale

Survey respondents overwhelmingly favor the upper half of a numerical happiness scale. In 2016–2019, on the GWP scale of zero to 10, 82 percent chose values of 5 or greater. On the slightly shorter EVS scale of 1–10, 81 percent answered 6 or more. In the Gallup survey, the happiness value most often chosen is 5 or 7; in the EVS survey, 8 (Figure 4).

Both the GWP and EVS frequency distributions of happiness have a bump at the happiness response value of 5, reflecting the tendency of some respondents to choose the midpoint of an integer scale. The bump is much more pronounced in the Gallup responses where on the 11-point scale of 0–10, the midpoint is

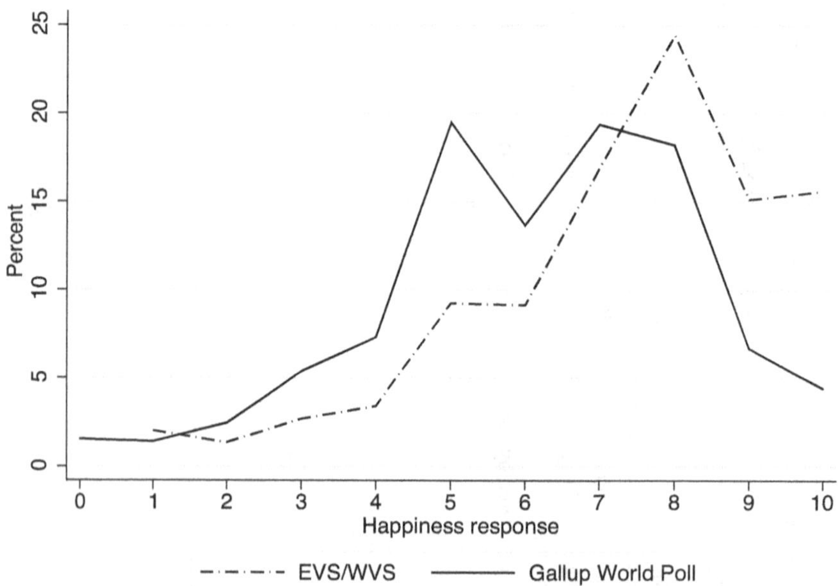

Figure 4 Percent with indicated happiness response: GWP Best Possible Life, mean of thirty-seven countries, 2016–2019, and EVS Life Satisfaction, mean of thirty-one countries, 2017–2019.

Source: Author calculations, Gallup World Poll (Gallup, 2020) and EVS/WVS (EVS, 2015, 2020; Haerpfer et al., 2020; Inglehart et al., 2018).

Table 11 Mean happiness, percent responding five or more, and happiness Gini by region, 2016–2019

Region	(1) Number of countries	(2) Mean happiness	(3) Percent 5+	(4) Happiness Gini
Europe	37	6.19	82.1	0.173
Western Bloc	16	6.94	91.5	0.133
Northern	4	7.57	95.6	0.108
Western	8	7.11	94.2	0.121
Southern	4	5.98	82.1	0.183
Eastern Bloc	21	5.61	74.9	0.204
Central and Eastern	12	5.77	77.2	0.199
Former Soviet Union	9	5.39	71.7	0.209

Note: Average values calculated by country and then by region across countries. The happiness measure is the GWP Best Possible Life.
Source: Author calculations, Gallup World Poll (Gallup, 2020).

clearly centered at 5, while the 10-point EVS scale leaves the midpoint more ambiguous. Hence, there is a somewhat smoother response distribution in EVS surveys compared with Gallup.

The tendency to favor the upper half of the response scale is true in all geographic regions at every date, and, not surprisingly, the higher the proportion in the upper half, the higher is happiness (Table 11, columns 2 and 3). For the full set of thirty-seven countries in the GWP in 2016–2019, the correlation coefficient between mean happiness and the proportion with happiness responses of 5 or more is 0.97; for the thirty-one countries in the EVS, the correlation coefficient between mean happiness and the proportion responding 6 or more is 0.94. Both coefficients are highly significant.

4.2 Inequality in Happiness among Persons

Typically, as more and more persons move into the upper half of the happiness distribution and become increasingly bunched there, happiness differences among persons lessen. As differences in happiness among persons decrease, mean happiness increases.

A "*happiness* Gini" coefficient, whose values range from zero to one, provides a summary measure of the magnitude of happiness differences among persons, a smaller Gini signifying greater equality. It is calculated here for each country from the frequency distribution of the population ranked from low to high according to *happiness*.[7] It differs from the Gini used in Section 3 to summarize income inequality, which used differences in income, not happiness, and the population ranked according to size of income, not happiness.

Data for the individual European regions for 2016–2019 demonstrate the inverse relationship between the happiness Gini and mean happiness – a smaller Gini going with higher mean happiness and also with a larger proportion in the top half of the happiness distribution (Table 11, compare column 4 with columns 2 and 3). In the Northern region, where happiness and the proportion in the top half are highest, the Gini is the lowest, 0.108, signifying the greatest equality in happiness among persons. In the countries of the Former Soviet Union, where mean happiness and respondents in the top segment are lowest, the Gini is the highest, 0.209, indicating the largest inequality in happiness among persons. As we have seen, for the thirty-seven individual countries the correlation coefficient between mean happiness and the proportion 5+ is 0.97; the correlation between mean happiness and the happiness Gini is a highly significant –0.94.

4.3 Evolution and Importance of Happiness Inequality

Over the nearly forty-year period from 1981 to 2018, happiness inequality declined in all but four of the twelve countries for which we have long-run data (Table 12). Three countries from Northern Europe – Denmark, Finland, and Sweden – experienced a small increase in the happiness Gini, however, they were already at low levels of inequality in the 1980s, and remained the least unequal in 2017–2019 (Table 11). Russia, on the other hand, experienced a substantial increase in inequality. Taking the data for the Russian oblast of Tambov as a proxy for Russia, as discussed in Section 2, Tambov had greater happiness equality in 1982 than both Italy and France, but by 2018, Russia was the least equal of the twelve countries. It seems that the collapse of the socialist greenhouse, mentioned in Section 3, contributed to a significant decline in both the average level of happiness as well as the equality of its distribution.

This decline in happiness inequality was associated with increasing average happiness. Indeed, in changes over time as well as at a point-of-time, mean happiness and happiness inequality among persons are inversely related. On each line of Table 12, the signs for changes in mean happiness and happiness Gini are the opposite of each other, with only one exception, the Eastern

[7] Although there is some disagreement about how to measure happiness inequality (Delhey and Kohler, 2011; Kalmijn and Veenhoven, 2005), in the present case, the distinction between the happiness Gini and standard deviation of happiness is minimal as they are correlated at about 95 percent.

Table 12 Change in mean happiness and in happiness Gini, by region, 1981–1982 to 2017–2018

Region	Change in happiness	Change in happiness Gini
All	**0.13**	**−0.016**
Western Bloc	**0.22**	**−0.019**
Northern	**−0.14**	**0.002**
Norway	0.12	−0.017
Sweden	−0.37	0.008
Finland	−0.01	0.014
Denmark	−0.31	0.004
Western	**0.29**	**−0.018**
Great Britain	0.05	−0.013
France	0.60	−0.032
Netherlands	0.13	−0.011
Germany	0.39	−0.015
Southern	**0.77**	**−0.063**
Spain	0.89	−0.049
Italy	0.66	−0.078
Eastern Bloc	**−0.30**	**−0.003**
Central and Eastern	**0.22**	**−0.031**
Hungary	0.22	−0.031
Former Soviet Union	**−0.83**	**0.025**
Russia	−0.83	0.025

Note: The happiness measure is EVS Life Satisfaction.
Source: Author calculations, EVS/WVS (EVS, 2015, 2020; Haerpfer et al., 2020; Inglehart et al., 2018).

Bloc average. Across countries, the correlation between the change in mean happiness and the change in the happiness Gini is –0.87, significant at 1 percent.

Happiness inequality is a growing cause of concern. As an example, in 2018 the U.K.'s Office of National Statistics commissioned the New Economics Foundation to ascertain the best measure of happiness inequality to report to the U.K. public alongside average happiness. The authors found that key stakeholders and the public dislike inequality and prefer to improve the lives of the least happy more than the rest; this means that, in the United Kingdom, three hypothetical countries with equal average happiness are not equally desirable to live in. The most desirable country is the one with a more equal distribution of happiness and with fewer people at the extreme low end of the distribution. The middle country could have the same happiness inequality but more extremely unhappy people, while the least desirable has either the greatest inequality or the greatest number of unhappy people. This preference is reminiscent of the work of political philosopher John Rawls. In a famous thought experiment, John Rawls asked people to imagine themselves behind a "veil of ignorance," without knowledge of their life circumstances, and imagine the kind of society that they would want to live in (Rawls, 1971). Behind such a veil, risk-averse people would choose to live in a society with more happiness equality (Clark et al., 2014).

Among the few studies that have looked at happiness inequality, two have pointed to both economic growth and the expansion of the social safety net as potential determinants (Clark et al., 2016, 2014). However, in our case, neither is correlated with changes in the happiness Gini. Another natural candidate is income inequality, yet as shown in Section 3, income inequality generally grew in these countries, and the correlation is also statistically insignificant. Clark et al. (2016, 2014) also point to psychological mechanisms, such as changing reference levels and social comparison, but ultimately concluded that the decline in happiness inequality is difficult to explain. Once more, more research is necessary.

5 Happiness Differences among Demographic Groups

The previous section looked at happiness differences among individuals. In this section, the focus is on happiness differences when persons are grouped according to various personal characteristics. Thus, we ask: on average, are the rich happier than the poor, men happier than women, the young happier than the old, native born happier than the foreign born, city-folk happier than rural?

5.1 Happiness Differences by Socio-Economic Status

People with higher socio-economic status (SES) tend to be happier than people with lower SES – the rich are, indeed, happier, on average than the poor at a point in time. This is due in part to the benefits of additional education, health, and income, which all tend to go together for the higher SES, and also partly to the influence of social comparison. Persons in the top quartile of the income distribution are happier than persons in the next quartile (Table 13). The bottom quartile is the least happy. This holds in each region, but the differences between groups are most pronounced in Southern Europe and the Central and Eastern European countries.

Table 13 Happiness, mean and by income quartile, and happiness/SES Gini, by region, 2016–2019

Region	(1) Number of countries	(2) Mean happiness	(3) Bottom quartile	(4) 26–50%	(5) 51–75%	(6) Top quartile	(7) Happiness/ SES Gini
Europe	37	6.19	5.65	6.02	6.35	6.74	0.041
Western Bloc	16	6.94	6.44	6.85	7.13	7.37	0.029
Northern	4	7.57	7.25	7.49	7.71	7.84	0.018
Western	8	7.11	6.59	7.06	7.30	7.50	0.025
Southern	4	5.98	5.31	5.77	6.21	6.64	0.047
Eastern Bloc	21	5.61	5.05	5.39	5.75	6.26	0.050
Central and Eastern	12	5.77	5.14	5.58	5.94	6.45	0.051
Former Soviet Union	9	5.39	4.92	5.14	5.51	5.99	0.048

Note: Average values calculated by country and then by region across countries. The happiness measure is the GWP Best Possible Life. The Happiness-SES Gini uses the unweighted income distribution.

Source: Author calculations, Gallup World Poll (Gallup, 2020).

The relationship between income and happiness is fairly complex. It differs when comparing different people at a *point-of-time* from the relation based on changes *over time*. This is due largely to two psychological processes that affect the internal reference levels used by individuals to evaluate their lives (cf. Section 1). According to social comparison, people experience greater happiness when they compare their status to those of lower status and vice-versa. This partially explains why the rich are happier than the poor in Table 13. The second process is adaptation. People tend to adjust their reference levels as they adapt or habituate to higher incomes over time. Consequently, the direct benefits of income, accruing to higher SES, tend to diminish over time as people adapt.

Some countries experience greater happiness differences between SES groups than others, which relates to the overall level of happiness in a country. Countries that have greater happiness equality between the more and less affluent, or smaller happiness gaps between income quartiles, tend to be happier (Table 13). The quartiles may hide some important differences, however; for example, between the top 1st and 10th percentiles of the income distribution. To account for this heterogeneity, we construct another happiness Gini, this time calculating the mean value of happiness when the population is ranked according to income. The resulting happiness-SES Gini contrasts the happiness of persons for each level of income; the *"happiness* Gini" from Section 4 contrasts happiness among persons when ranked according to their happiness, not income.

The gap in happiness between the more and less affluent according to the happiness-SES Gini is lowest in the Northern and Western regions (Table 13). The happiness-SES Gini is highest in the Southern and Eastern Bloc regions. These results are similar to those in the previous section. Each of the three regions with high happiness-SES Ginis also has larger differences among individuals as measured by the happiness Gini (Table 12). In general, the happiness Gini and happiness-SES Gini are highly correlated at 0.87. Thus, whether using happiness or income groups, greater equality is accompanied by greater national happiness.

5.2 Differences Between Women and Men

Women, in general, have more adverse life circumstances than men – lower incomes, greater likelihood of widowhood, and worse reported health – all of which would tend to reduce women's happiness relative to men. Women also tend to report lower *affective* subjective well-being, for example, higher depression and anxiety (Blanchflower and Bryson, 2022). But in EVS surveys dating from 1981 on, women and men evaluate their subjective well-being about equally in almost every country in both the Western and Eastern Blocs. The difference in happiness between women and men across countries is almost always less than 0.2 points on a scale of 1–10 (Table 14). The surprisingly high relative happiness of women is a worldwide phenomenon (Blanchflower and Bryson, 2022; Zweig, 2014), which might be explained by different response styles, aspirations, or reference levels compared to men (Montgomery, 2022).

However, the near equality of happiness of women and men for all ages taken together conceals a notable and virtually universal difference in their comparative happiness at younger and older ages. Typically, women are happier than men up to retirement age, but thereafter men are happier. This reversal is found in every region (Table 14). Retirement from the labor force, which has a positive impact on happiness, tends to be more important for men, because they typically have had greater labor force participation. Another important reason for the reversal in the gender difference in happiness at younger and older ages is the gender difference in whether one is living with a partner, a household arrangement that contributes to higher happiness. At younger ages women are more likely than men to have a partner, while at older ages, the opposite is true (Plagnol and Easterlin, 2008).

5.3 Happiness Differences by Age and Cohort

At a point in time, happiness at older ages tends to be less than at younger ages, with the oldest age group being the least happy. This is what one would expect because older persons tend to be less healthy and less likely to be living with a partner, circumstances that diminish happiness. The lower happiness of the old is a common feature of both Western and Eastern Bloc countries (Table 15). In Eastern Bloc countries, the happiness decline with age tends to occur consistently from one age group to the next. In the Western Bloc countries, however, upward movements often interrupt the generally downward trend.

These point-of-time happiness differences by age should not be considered indicative of life course experience, however, because the different age groups comprise different birth cohorts (or generations) with different lifetime experiences. In 2018, for example, the age group 18–24 consists of individuals born in 1996–2000 ("generation Z"), while the 75–84 year-olds hail from 1934 to 1943 (the "silent generation"). This means, for example, that in Eastern Bloc countries the younger age group would have largely escaped the vicissitudes of the transition from socialism to capitalism experienced by the older group (Easterlin, 2010).

Table 14 Mean happiness by gender and region, specified ages, 2016–2019

Region	Gender	All ages	Ages 25–64	Ages 65+
Europe	Women	6.18	6.24	5.65
	Men	6.19	6.17	5.80
Western Bloc	Women	6.94	7.00	6.72
	Men	6.95	6.94	6.87
Northern	Women	7.62	7.67	7.55
	Men	7.52	7.49	7.56
Western	Women	7.11	7.15	6.99
	Men	7.12	7.11	7.11
Southern	Women	5.94	6.04	5.34
	Men	6.03	6.03	5.70
Eastern Bloc	Women	5.60	5.65	4.84
	Men	5.61	5.58	4.98
Central and Eastern	Women	5.77	5.82	5.00
	Men	5.78	5.75	5.16
Former Soviet Union	Women	5.38	5.43	4.62
	Men	5.39	5.35	4.75

Note: Average values calculated by country and then by region across countries. The happiness measure is GWP Best Possible Life.
Source: Author calculations, Gallup World Poll (Gallup, 2020).

A more accurate picture of happiness over the life course is obtained by a multiple regression that includes controls for birth cohort and time. A regression separates out the influence of birth cohort by using a dummy variable for each birth cohort, which captures the influence of the period in which each respondent was born. Survey-wave dummies were likewise used to control for the time period in which each survey was conducted.

The regression results reveal striking differences across the Eastern and Western Blocs. In the Eastern Bloc, happiness declines with age (Table 16, column 3), consistent with the age patterns in Table 15. Each age group draws a statistically significant and negative coefficient, which indicates those respondents are less happy than the reference group, 18–24 years old, and the coefficients increase in size (more negative) as people age. The respondents who are seventy-five or more years old are nearly one point less happy compared to those who are 18–24 (0.99 on a 1–10 scale, Table 16, column 3). While in the Western Bloc, happiness only declines into middle age, ages 45–54, and then returns in older ages to the levels observed at ages 18–24 – statistically, happiness in ages 55 and above is indistinguishable from happiness experienced

Table 15 Mean happiness, population 15+, by age group and region, 2016–2019

Region	All ages	15–17	18–24	25–34	35–44	45–54	55–64	65–74	75+
Europe	6.19	6.95	6.65	6.41	6.31	6.16	5.91	5.81	5.51
Western Bloc	6.94	7.32	7.03	6.98	7.02	6.99	6.87	6.89	6.56
Northern	7.57	7.97	7.48	7.51	7.55	7.63	7.63	7.66	7.37
Western	7.11	7.19	7.10	7.09	7.16	7.16	7.13	7.14	6.85
Southern	5.98	6.93	6.45	6.26	6.20	6.01	5.62	5.62	5.16
Eastern Bloc	5.61	6.67	6.36	5.98	5.77	5.53	5.17	5.00	4.71
Central and Eastern	5.77	6.89	6.57	6.17	5.97	5.70	5.33	5.16	4.92
Former Soviet Union	5.39	6.39	6.08	5.73	5.52	5.32	4.95	4.78	4.42

Note: Average values calculated by country and then by region across countries. The happiness measure is GWP Best Possible Life.
Source: Gallup World Poll, (Gallup, 2020).

at ages 18–24. (Table 16, column 2). This pattern resembles the commonly observed U-shape that happiness takes with age, in which youth and old age are the happiest stages in life (Blanchflower and Oswald, 2008). However, when age groups beyond 70 are distinguished, typically a decline in happiness is observed, reflecting the negative impact of poorer health and loss of a partner (Morgan and O'Connor, 2017, 2020). This decline is somewhat visible in the Western Bloc, as the coefficient on the 75 plus is negative, compared to the reference group, but not statistically significant. While in the Eastern Bloc, the 75 plus are less happy than every previous age (Table 16, columns 2 and 3).

The regression results also reveal differences across generations (Table 16). Across the Eastern and Western Blocs, the older generations tend to be less happy, but only the Greatest Generation in the Western Bloc is statistically less happy than the Baby Boomers. In the Eastern Bloc, younger generations tend to be happier. Of particular note, the oft-discussed Millennials (born 1980–1994) are happier than their parents in the Eastern Bloc, and by a meaningful amount, 0.34 points on a 1–10 scale. In the Western Bloc, the Millennials are not worse off than their parents.

5.4 Differences between Native and Foreign-Born Persons

The native born tend to be happier than the foreign born in every region of Europe (Table 17, column 5), by 0.22 points on average. This tendency holds in all but a few exceptional countries. One notable exception is Portugal, which experienced a substantial inflow of Brazilians, whose happiness on average exceeded that of the native Portuguese. Another outlier was Finland which has a much smaller proportion of foreign born than Western Bloc countries generally, only about 7 percent. There, the happiness of the foreign born, largely Russians, Estonians, and Swedes, is about the same as that of the native Finns. The other three countries in which the foreign-born are happier (Bosnia and Herzegovina, Georgia, and Hungary) also have low population shares of foreign-born. In Bosnia and Herzegovina, the foreign-born share is only one percent of the total population.

The native-foreign born happiness gap is due in part to substantial differences in national policies to protect and assist migrants. The strength of these national policies is measured here by MIPEX, an index ranging from a low of 0 to 100, with higher values indicating stronger policies (Table 17 column 6, (Solano and Huddleston, 2021)). The relations support what we might expect – in general, stronger policies narrow the gap between natives and the foreign born. The correlation between the native-foreign born happiness gap and MIPEX score is –0.40. This is visible across regions. Northern European countries have the

Table 16 Regression of happiness on age and birth cohort

	(1) Europe		(2) Western Bloc		(3) Eastern Bloc	
	Coefficient	***p*-value**	**Coefficient**	***p*-value**	**Coefficient**	***p*-value**
Age 18–24	Reference		Reference		Reference	
Age 25–34	−0.170***	(0.000)	−0.103**	(0.017)	−0.209***	(0.000)
Age 35–44	−0.329***	(0.000)	−0.146**	(0.040)	−0.393***	(0.000)
Age 45–54	−0.493***	(0.000)	−0.236***	(0.002)	−0.600***	(0.000)
Age 55–64	−0.458***	(0.000)	−0.072	(0.409)	−0.661***	(0.000)
Age 65–74	−0.503***	(0.000)	0.069	(0.491)	−0.849***	(0.000)
Age 75+	−0.622***	(0.000)	−0.023	(0.864)	−0.989***	(0.000)
Greatest: Born <1925	0.015	(0.883)	−0.272*	(0.052)	−0.023	(0.875)
Silent: Born 1925–1945	−0.034	(0.428)	−0.056	(0.273)	−0.024	(0.623)
Baby Boomers: Born 1946–1964	Reference		Reference		Reference	
Generation X: Born 1965–1979	0.069*	(0.056)	0.015	(0.689)	0.149***	(0.006)
Millennials: Born 1980–1994	0.154**	(0.023)	−0.014	(0.867)	0.335***	(0.000)

Table 16 (cont.)

	(1)		(2)		(3)	
	Europe		Western Bloc		Eastern Bloc	
	Coefficient	***p*-value**	**Coefficient**	***p*-value**	**Coefficient**	***p*-value**
Constant	6.161***	(0.000)	7.580***	(0.000)	5.497***	(0.000)
Country and wave dummies	Yes		Yes		Yes	
Number of observations	154,026		66,382		87,644	
R-squared	0.165		0.050		0.153	

The regression is based on the EVS data from 1996 to 2019 for the full set of thirty-seven countries (only a smaller subset of countries extends back to the 1980s), includes age and birth cohort categories, and country and wave dummies. Respondents that were 15–17 years old or born after 1994 were dropped due to small sample sizes.

Standard errors clustered by country; * $p < 0.10$ ** $p < 0.05$ *** $p < 0.01$.

Source: Author calculations, EVS/WVS (EVS, 2015, 2020; Haerpfer et al., 2020; Inglehart et al., 2018).

Table 17 Mean happiness by nativity and region, and integration policy, 2016–2019

	(1)	(2)	(3)	(4)	(5)	(6)
Region	**Count[a]**	**All**	**Native born**	**Foreign born**	**Native – Foreign Gap**	**Integration Policy[b]**
Europe	34	6.26	6.28	6.06	0.22	53.03
Western Bloc	16	6.94	6.97	6.75	0.21	60.81
Northern	4	7.57	7.57	7.49	0.08	72.75
Western	8	7.11	7.15	6.82	0.33	55.00
Southern	4	5.98	5.99	5.87	0.12	60.50
Eastern Bloc	18	5.66	5.67	5.44	0.23	44.14
Central and Eastern	9	5.93	5.93	5.86	0.07	44.75
Former Soviet Union	9	5.39	5.41	5.02	0.39	43.33

Note: Average values calculated by country and then by region across countries. The happiness measure is GWP Best Possible Life. Integration Policy ranges from 0 to 100 with higher scores representing better treatment of foreign born.

[a] The number of countries for which reliable foreign-born happiness data are available. Three Central and Eastern countries were excluded due to a low number of foreign-born observations: Romania, Bulgaria, and Albania. Additional countries were missing in the MIPEX data.

[b] The score is not available for the Central and Eastern European countries, Bosnia and Herzegovina, and the Former Soviet Countries: Belarus, Georgia, and Armenia. Romania, Bulgaria, and Albania are also dropped because they are missing the happiness data.

Source: Author calculations (Gallup, 2020; Solano and Huddleston, 2021).

strongest policies and the smallest gap, while the Former Soviet Union countries have the weakest policies and largest gap. The Central and Eastern countries are somewhat anomalous here, exhibiting weak policies and a low gap.

There are substantial differences in the shares of foreign-born across regions. Most striking is the notable difference between the Western and Eastern Blocs. In the Western Bloc, the foreign-born proportion is high, ranging from 10 to 17 percent (Table 18, column 2). In the Eastern Bloc, the corresponding figure is much less, typically around 7–8 percent.

As suggested earlier, countries with a lower share of foreign-born tend to have a lower native-foreign born happiness gap. There are some regional exceptions, for instance, Northern Europe has a larger foreign-born share and

Table 18 Total foreign born population share, disaggregated by place of birth, 2019

	(1)	(2)	(3)	(4)	(5)	(6)	(7)	(8)
			Percent of foreign-born by origin region					
Region	**Count[a]**	**FB Pop. Share**	**West**	**North**	**South**	**Cen. & East**	**FSU**	**Non-Europe**
Europe	**34**	**10.91**	**9.78**	**1.77**	**3.41**	**25.81**	**26.39**	**32.85**
Western Bloc	**16**	**14.86**	**14.94**	**3.16**	**6.04**	**18.86**	**7.16**	**49.85**
Northern Europe	4	13.77	8.45	10.81	2.78	13.42	10.54	54.01
Western Europe	8	17.41	18.51	0.65	9.51	19.27	4.47	47.60
Southern Europe	4	10.83	14.30	0.52	2.36	23.48	9.15	50.20
Eastern Bloc	**18**	**7.40**	**5.19**	**0.53**	**1.08**	**31.99**	**43.48**	**17.73**
Central and Eastern Europe	9	6.59	8.64	0.37	1.38	63.12	12.94	13.55
Former Soviet Union	9	8.22	1.73	0.69	0.79	0.86	74.02	21.91

Foreign-born individuals include anyone legally residing in a country that is not their place of birth; this definition includes naturalized migrants who have become citizens where they reside. Different countries have different rules for reporting citizenship figures, on dual citizenship for instance, which would limit consistent analysis using alternative definitions. The Czech Republic is an exception. There, the foreign-born only include noncitizen residents – foreign-born peoples that have become naturalized citizens are considered natives. Displaced peoples seeking asylum have a temporary legal status and are not included in foreign-born numbers until they have been granted the right to stay. Hungary, Bosnia and Herzegovina, and Croatia are exceptions. Their figures include refugees.

[a] The number of countries for which reliable foreign-born happiness data are available. Three Central and Eastern countries were excluded due to a low number of foreign-born observations: Romania, Bulgaria, and Albania.

Source: Author calculations, (United Nations Population Division, 2019).

a smaller happiness gap compared to Southern Europe. However, across all countries, there is a positive correlation of 20 percent. This result, in which greater population shares of foreign born are associated with greater happiness gaps, is somewhat surprising. One draw, or pull factor, for migrants to choose one destination over another is the number of other foreign-born like them in the destination country (Beine et al., 2011), which suggests that the foreign-born are happier in countries with a higher foreign-born share.

The differences in the size and composition of the foreign-born populations reflect the varied net migration streams both within and from outside of Europe in recent decades. In many Western Bloc countries, there were substantial inflows from Asia and Africa, partly reflecting movements from former colonies, and partly due to disruptions abroad caused by war, civil conflict, and/or political oppression. In the Western Bloc, the proportion of all foreign-born accounted for by non-Europeans is almost three times that in the Eastern Bloc, nearly fifty compared to 18 percent (Table 18, column 8). There were also sizeable movements of Europeans from the Eastern Bloc to the Western Bloc, particularly in connection with the accession of countries to the European Union. Especially noteworthy in this respect were outflows from Poland and Romania to the Western Bloc.

In the Eastern Bloc, the largest migrations have typically been related to the partition of the pre-World War II nations of Yugoslavia, Czechoslovakia, and especially the Soviet Union. These break-ups very often set off movements of persons returning to the country of their ethnicity, for example, Slovaks returning from Czechia to Slovakia, Czechs emigrating from Slovakia to Czechia, and Russians moving from countries formerly part of the Soviet Union to the Russian Federation. More than 60 percent of the foreign born in the Central and Eastern region are from within that same region, and the number is even higher in the Former Soviet Union – nearly three out of every four foreign-born in the region are from within that region (Table 18, column 7).

5.5 Happiness Differences by Place of Residence

In Europe as a whole, there is little difference in happiness between urban and rural residents (Table 19, row 1). This contrasts with the worldwide pattern in which urban residents are typically happier than rural (Burger et al., 2020). Urban refers here to places of 20,000 population or more; rural, to places under 20,000, including persons living in the countryside.

This overall equality conceals, however, significant differences among the various parts of Europe. In most Eastern Bloc countries and in the Southern

Table 19 Mean happiness of population by size of place, 2017–2019

Region	< 20,000	20,000 to 100,000	> 100,000
Europe	7.27	7.30	7.29
Western Bloc	7.62	7.63	7.45
Northern	7.97	7.87	7.82
Western	7.80	7.71	7.49
Southern	6.94	7.18	6.89
Eastern Bloc	7.03	7.08	7.19
Central and Eastern	7.23	7.32	7.38
Former Soviet Union	6.67	6.65	6.83

Note: The happiness measure is EVS Life Satisfaction. Great Britain and the Netherlands are excluded because they do not have size of place data in the most recent period. Likewise, North Macedonia is excluded because it is missing data for respondents in cities larger than 100,000. The Gallup data give approximately the same results.
Source: Author calculations, EVS/WVS (EVS, 2015, 2020; Haerpfer et al., 2020; Inglehart et al., 2018).

region of the Western Bloc urban residents are typically happier than rural. But in the wealthiest part of Europe – the Northern and Western regions of the Western Bloc – rural residents tend to be happier (Table 19).

These disparate regional patterns of rural-urban happiness reflect chiefly the transformation of rural areas as the Industrial and Demographic Revolutions evolve (Easterlin et al., 2011). Historically, rural areas have been dominated by agricultural activity. Farming is typically the least happy occupation by far, and this chiefly explains the usual shortfall of rural vis-à-vis urban happiness, which still prevails in Southern Europe and the Eastern Bloc. In the twentieth century, the innovation of motor vehicles, and subsequently the computer, increased substantially the attractiveness of rural locations for the location of nonagricultural industry and household residence. In addition, the Demographic Revolution led to population aging and disproportionate growth of the retirement population. The location decisions of retirees, unconstrained by place of work, increasingly favor rural locations and attract supportive industries. The result of these several developments is a rural revival and with it a gradual reversal of the historic excess of urban over rural happiness. The Northern and Western regions of Europe have been the leaders in the Industrial and Demographic Revolutions and hence are the first to show rural happiness in excess of urban.

5.6 Long-Run Influence of Demographic Change

The demographic characteristics of Europe significantly changed over the past forty years. In all but one country of twelve, Hungary, the female population share declined relative to men (Table 20). In each country the population aged and people moved to cities. The old age dependency ratio, which is the population aged 65+ compared to the population 15–64, increased by nearly ten percentage points on average. In Italy, the ratio went from approximately 1 in 5 (21 percent) to more than 1 in 3 (36 percent). The largest increase in urbanization occurred in the Netherlands, where more than 90 percent of the population now lives in urban areas.

One might expect these shifts to have an impact on happiness and indeed there are some visible patterns across regions. Within the Western Bloc, Northern Europe tended to have a greater decline in the female population share, less population aging, fewer people move to cities (except compared to Southern Europe), and was the only Western Bloc region to experience a decline in happiness (Table 20). But across countries, all of the correlations are insignificant. The relative decline in women, increase in population aged 65+, and share of people living in urban areas did not systematically relate to changing happiness, positively or negatively.

Migration is another demographic characteristic that could have plausibly affected happiness. However, we refrain from analyzing the change in the number of foreign-born and emigrants here because the analysis is too involved to cover in a short section. For example, it may be surprising[8] to some to learn that countries that have a greater foreign-born population share are happier (O'Connor, 2020), however, that is a cross-sectional result, which is driven in part by the fact that migrants tend to move to happier places (Grimes and Wesselbaum, 2021, 2019). This means migration may affect happiness, but happiness also affects migration, which complicates the analysis. What is more, countries are affected both by the people who move in as well as by those who move out, and migration affects a host of characteristics, including for instance: social cohesion, wages, cost of production, diversity of goods and services, brain drain, and remittances.

A few existing studies suggest that the impacts in origin and destination countries are fairly small, including economic (Clemens, 2011; Dustmann et al., 2016) and happiness impacts (Hendriks and Burger, 2021; O'Connor, 2020); however, there are some recent studies that document varying relations. In two recent studies, the authors find more open and trusting U.K. natives experience positive effects of immigration, while more closed and distrusting natives experience negative effects (Howley and Waqas, 2024).

[8] Given the generally negative media coverage of immigration.

Table 20 Changes in mean happiness and demographic characteristics by Region, 1981–1982 to 2017–2018

Region	(1) Life sat. (1– 10)	(2) Female share % of Tot. Pop.	(3) Old age dep. %	(4) Urbanization %
All	**0.13**	**−0.35**	**9.23**	**7.92**
Western Bloc	**0.22**	**−0.49**	**9.62**	**8.46**
Northern	**−0.14**	**−0.71**	**8.15**	**8.00**
Norway	0.12	−0.97	2.23	11.33
Sweden	−0.37	−0.58	5.91	4.05
Finland	−0.01	−0.90	16.11	12.80
Denmark	−0.31	−0.37	8.33	3.84
Western	**0.29**	**−0.51**	**9.34**	**10.54**
Great Britain	0.05	−0.72	5.40	4.81
France	0.60	0.38	10.81	7.09
Netherlands	0.13	−0.14	11.74	25.97
Germany	0.39	−1.59	9.40	4.27
Southern	**0.77**	**−0.01**	**13.11**	**5.20**
Spain	0.89	−0.01	11.17	6.80
Italy	0.66	−0.01	15.05	3.60
Eastern Bloc	**−0.30**	**0.36**	**7.31**	**5.23**
Central and Eastern	**0.22**	**0.80**	**8.70**	**6.80**
Hungary	0.22	0.80	8.70	6.80
Former Soviet Union	**−0.83**	**−0.08**	**5.92**	**3.66**
Russia	−0.83	−0.08	5.92	3.66

Note: The happiness measure is EVS Life Satisfaction. Old Age Dep. is ratio of the population older than 64 compared the population aged 15–64. Urbanization is the population share that lives in urban areas as defined by national statistical offices.
Source: Author calculation, EVS/WVS (EVS, 2015, 2020; Haerpfer et al., 2020; Inglehart et al., 2018). World Development Indicators (World Bank, 2020).

6 COVID-19 Postscript[9]

Since 2019, happiness in every country in Europe has been adversely affected by the COVID-19 pandemic. Although the focus of this Element is long-term trends in happiness, a brief update is appropriate in the light of this dramatic and

[9] This section is based on previous work conducted by the authors (Easterlin and O'Connor, 2023).

unforeseen event. In what follows we first provide evidence of the geographic range of the pandemic and then describe its impact on happiness. For our measure of happiness, we shift to the Eurobarometer, with its 1–4 scale, mentioned in Section 1, because of its availability on a semiannual basis. The shortcomings of the Eurobarometer mentioned in Section 2 apply to periods longer than the three years studied here.

6.1 Geographic Scope of the Pandemic

No country in Europe has been able to escape the pandemic. This is apparent from the cumulative number of confirmed cases reported in each of the countries of Europe as of autumn 2022 (Table 21, column 1). On a per million population basis, the cumulative number of confirmed cases in Europe as a whole is well over 300,000, that is, more than three cases for every ten persons. Even in countries with the fewest reported cases, the number amounts to more than one case in ten.

Table 21 COVID-19: Cumulative confirmed cases and cumulative confirmed deaths per million population, Europe and subdivisions, March 2020–October 2022

	(1)	**(2)**
Place	**Cumulative Cases**	**Cumulative Deaths**
Europe	**337,961**	**2,828**
Western Bloc	**414,730**	**2,068**
Northern Europe	**331,651**	**1,271**
Norway	270,913	769
Sweden*	248,862	1,953
Finland*	239,064	1,128
Denmark*	567,765	1,234
Western Europe	**451,471**	**2,117**
United Kingdom*	353,722	3,091
Ireland*	334,978	1,606
France*	541,084	2,318
Netherlands*	485,581	1,305
Belgium*	395,674	2,826
Germany*	419,690	1,824
Austria*	601,865	2,348
Switzerland	479,173	1,616
Southern Europe	**424,326**	**2,766**
Spain*	283,501	2,414

Table 21 (cont.)

Place	(1) Cumulative Cases	(2) Cumulative Deaths
Portugal*	535,410	2,442
Italy*	391,863	3,009
Greece*	486,530	3,200
Eastern Bloc	**279,471**	**3,408**
Central and Eastern	**270,919**	**3,780**
Poland*	165,264	3,080
Czech Republic*	394,619	3,944
Slovak Republic*	484,365	3,769
Hungary*	219,623	4,923
Romania*	169,783	3,474
Bulgaria*	184,820	5,491
Slovenia*	576,051	3,239
Croatia*	306,125	4,198
Bosnia & Herzeg.	122,162	4,941
Albania	116,545	1,258
North Macedonia	163,467	4,543
Serbia	348,211	2,498
Former Soviet Union	**290,873**	**2,912**
Russia	144,940	2,628
Estonia*	455,800	2,054
Latvia*	504,874	3,221
Lithuania*	453,425	3,362
Belarus	103,782	743
Ukraine	128,258	2,703
Moldova	193,544	3,880
Armenia	159,396	3,119
Georgia	473,843	4,497

Source: Author calculations, Our World in Data (Mathieu et al., 2022).
* Countries included in the Eurobarometer Surveys.

The geographic scope of confirmed deaths per million (Table 21, column 2) is generally consistent with that of confirmed cases in showing a noticeable impact of the pandemic in every country. In the subsequent analysis of the effect of COVID-19 on happiness we rely primarily on the deaths measure, because it is more indicative of the severity of the COVID impact.

The numbers for cases and deaths in Table 21 understate substantially the magnitude of the pandemic. It is widely agreed that the true number of cases must be considerably more, because to qualify as a confirmed case there must be laboratory confirmation of infection. In regard to confirmed deaths, laboratory confirmation is not necessary, but the judgment of medical practitioners must be that the signs and symptoms point toward COVID-19 as the underlying cause of death. We cannot make much of differences in cases or deaths among individual countries, because COVID-19 reporting varies among countries due to differences in such things as COVID-19 definitions, case detection, laboratory testing, and reporting lag times in the underlying cause of death.

6.2 Temporal Pattern of the Pandemic

There are three complete COVID-19 waves from the start of the pandemic around the beginning of March 2020 to the autumn of 2022 (Figure 5). The first, a relatively short wave, extends from around March 2020 into the following summer and is comparatively mild, with a peak in April in deaths per million about half that of the subsequent two waves. The second wave stretches from the summer of 2020 to the summer of 2021, peaking in January 2021, and the third, from summer 2021 to the autumn of 2022 with a peak in December 2021. This is the picture for Europe as a whole; individual countries may, of course deviate from the general pattern, there being a slight tendency for Western Bloc countries to lead the Eastern Bloc.

The Eurobarometer surveys, whose fieldwork is usually 4–5 weeks in length, fall fortuitously at dates that provide a fairly good picture for the large second and third waves of the impact of COVID-19 on happiness in both the upswing and downswing of the pandemic. This can be seen in Figure 5 where vertical lines are drawn at the midpoint date of each of the six surveys spanning the period of the pandemic. For the first COVID-19 wave, the Eurobarometer survey interval that includes the wave is nine months long, about twice the duration of the wave itself, and includes the downswing along with the upswing. The happiness effect of the pandemic is consequently obscured. In what follows, therefore, we focus on the second and third waves.

In Europe as a whole in the second and third waves, the surge and relapse pattern of the pandemic in the successive intervals between the Eurobarometer surveys forms an M-pattern in COVID-19 deaths per million population (Figure 6, solid line). The right half of the M is somewhat less pronounced due to a substantial decline in deaths in the third wave compared to the second. Among the regions, this M-pattern is replicated in the two Eastern Bloc regions. In the Western Bloc, the first half of the M is seen in all three regions, but the

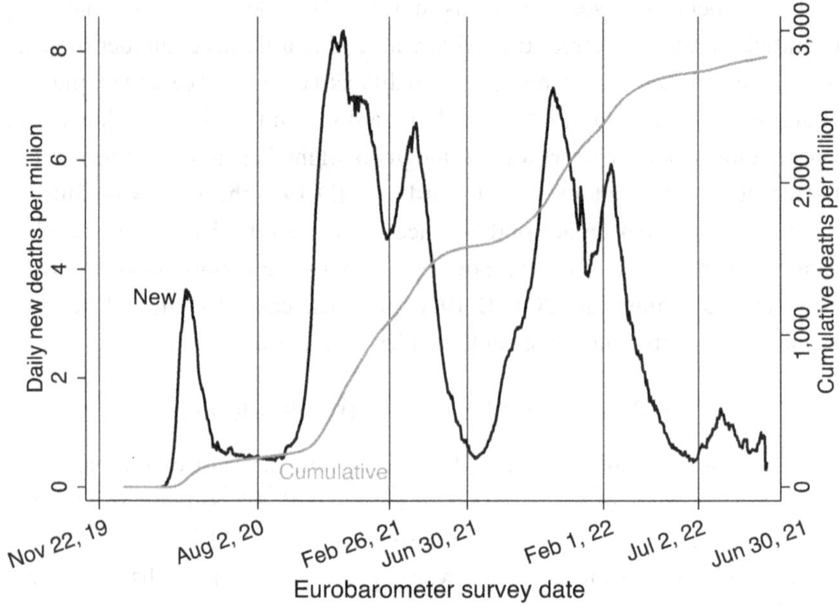

Figure 5 Daily new confirmed COVID-19 deaths and cumulative deaths per million, Europe, November 2019–August 2022.

Daily new and cumulative deaths are smoothed using a seven-day moving average. Vertical lines correspond to midpoints of Eurobarometer Survey Dates.

Source: Author calculations using data from Our World in Data (Mathieu et al., 2022).

second half is only faintly apparent in the Western and Southern regions and is nonexistent in the Northern region.

If the geographic coverage of deaths per million population is confined to the twenty-five countries for which Eurobarometer data on happiness are available (Figure 6, broken lines), the time-series patterns are virtually identical to those of Europe and its regions, making possible a comparison for these twenty-five countries of the COVID-19 and happiness patterns that is representative of Europe generally.

6.3 Impact of the Pandemic on Happiness

In every one of the twenty-five countries in the Eurobarometer surveys an upsurge in the pandemic has a negative impact on happiness in at least one and usually both of the second and third waves. Typically, an upsurge in COVID-19 deaths is matched by a decline in happiness and a downswing by an increase in happiness. Compared with happiness at the last pre-pandemic

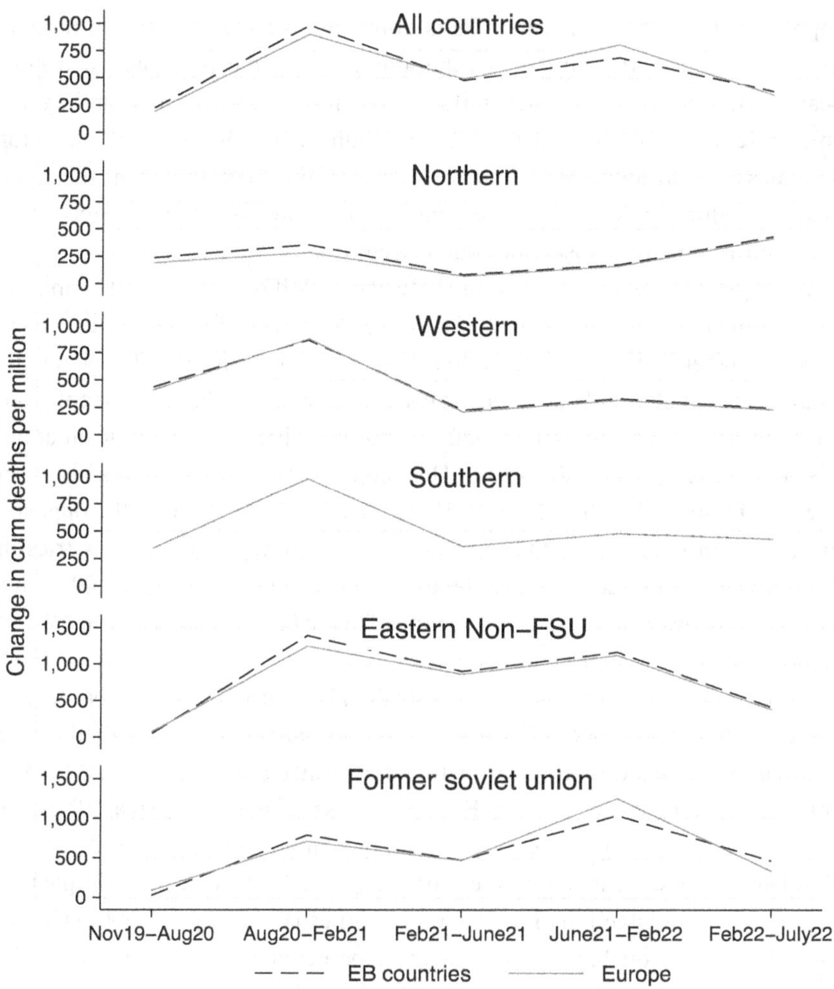

Figure 6 Change in number of deaths per million in successive eurobarometer survey intervals, Europe (solid line) and twenty-five Eurobarometer countries (dashed line), by region

For Southern region, both Europe and EB countries include the same four countries, so solid and dashed lines are the same.

Source: Author calculations, Our World in Data (Mathieu et al., 2022).

survey date in November 2019, happiness at the end of the third wave was, on average, about back to where it started.

At the regional level, the M-pattern for COVID-19 deaths (Figure 7, solid lines) tends to be matched by a W-shape for happiness (Figure 7, broken lines), indicative of the inverse relationship between deaths and happiness. In the second wave this is uniformly the case in all five regions of Europe, but in the third wave the amplitude of the movements in both deaths and happiness is much milder than in the second wave and varies among regions. In the third wave, the right wing of the W-pattern for happiness is still apparent in the two Eastern Bloc regions but in the three Western Bloc regions is either more moderate (in the Western and Southern regions) or absent (Northern region).

The typically negative relationship between COVID-19 deaths and happiness is confirmed by regression analysis. If for the twenty-five countries in the Eurobarometer surveys we regress the change in happiness in the four intervals from August 2020 to July 2022 on the change in deaths per hundred population, the result is an OLS regression coefficient of negative 1.018, significant at the $p < 0.01$ level (Table 22, col.1). This implies that happiness changes, on average, by just about the same amount as deaths per 100, but in the opposite direction. For example, in the twenty-five Eurobarometer survey countries in the upswing of the second wave the average change in deaths per 100 is just short of 0.10, and there is an equal decline of about 0.10 in happiness on the 1–4 response scale used in the Eurobarometer.

This decline of 0.10 in happiness is sizable. If we divide the Eurobarometer and EVS happiness scales of 1–4 and 1–10 into three equal parts, then on the 1–4 happiness scale of the Eurobarometer, a difference of 1 (e.g., 2–1) is equivalent on the more common EVS happiness scale of 1–10 to a difference that is three times as great (e.g., 4–1). So, the equivalent change to 0.1 on the Eurobarometer scale is 0.3 on the more common 1–10 scale. This impact on aggregate life satisfaction of 0.10 new deaths per 100 (or 1 per 1,000) is larger than the impact on happiness of a three-percentage point increase in the unemployment rate (Di Tella et al., 2001) and falls within the range of relations for individuals becoming unemployed or divorced (Helliwell et al., 2012).

These developments do not, of course, exhaust the factors impacting happiness in the second and third waves. To explore the many possible links is beyond the scope of this section, but it is worth noting one side effect of these new developments on preexisting COVID-19 policies. As the severity of the pandemic lessened noticeably and new deaths per million trended downward (Figure 8a), government containment and mitigation policies to reduce the impact of the pandemic were gradually relaxed. The extent of this easing is captured by the Stringency Index (Figure 8b). This is a summary measure of the magnitude and scope of restrictive government policies such as school and work shutdowns, stay-at-home requirements, and domestic and international travel restrictions. In

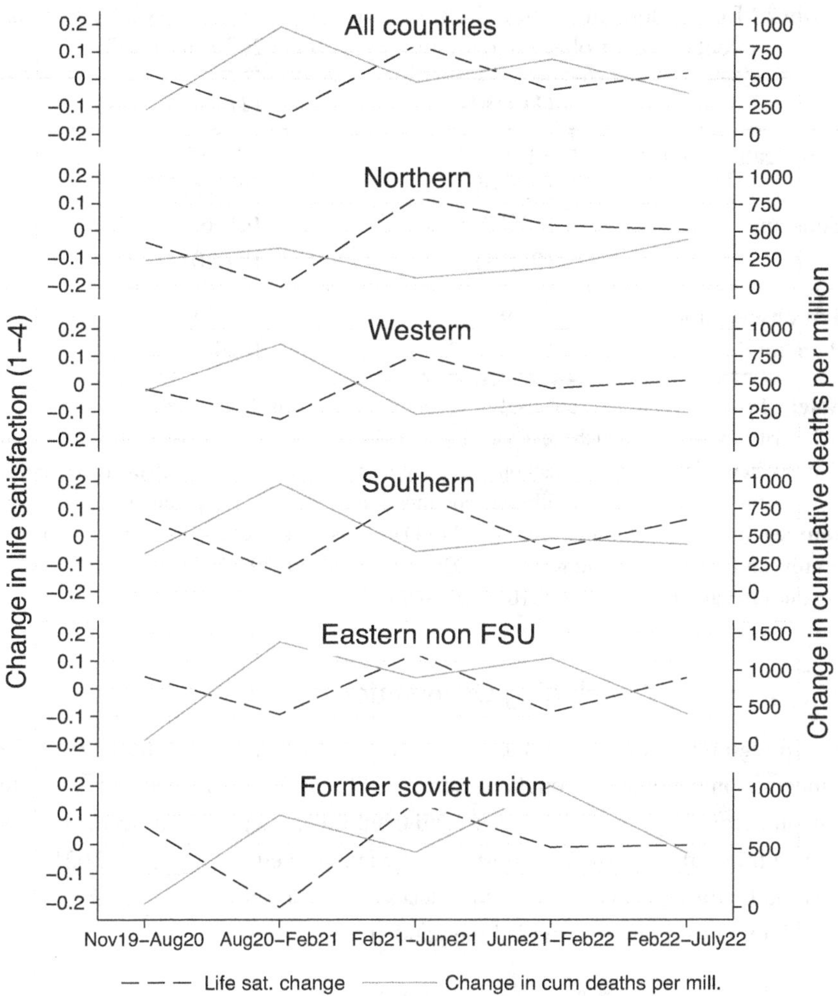

Figure 7 Number of deaths per million and change in Life Satisfaction in Successive Eurobarometer Survey Intervals, Eurobarometer Countries by Region

Source: Author calculations, Our World in Data (Mathieu et al., 2022); Eurobarometer (European Commission and Kantar, 2022a, 2022b, 2021a, 2021b, 2020, 2019)

turn, as restrictive policies were substantially eased, people resumed more normal lives, and time spent at recreation and retail locations returned to pre-pandemic levels (Figure 8c). This loosening of government restrictive policies, which previously reduced happiness (Clark and Lepinteur, 2022) added to the recovery in happiness.

Table 22 Regressions of changes in life satisfaction on new COVID-19 deaths twenty-five eurobarometer countries, August 2020–July 2022

	(1) OLS	**(2) FE**
New deaths per 100	−1.018***	−1 777***
	(0.259)	(0.311)
Constant	0.058***	0.106***
	(0.015)	(0.020)
# of observations	99	99
R-squared	0.132	0.244

Note: OLS – ordinary least squares. FE – country fixed effects. Life satisfaction is observed at five dates, as described in the text, yielding four observations per country of life satisfaction changes, new deaths. Life satisfaction is missing for the United Kingdom in the final survey. New deaths are per 100 (not million) in columns 1 and 2 to ease interpretation.
Source: Author calculations, Our World in Data (Mathieu et al., 2022); Eurobarometer (European Commission and Kantar, 2022a, 2022b, 2021a, 2021b, 2020, 2019).
p-values in parentheses: * $p < 0.10$ ** $p < 0.05$ *** $p < 0.01$.

6.4 Concluding Observations on COVID 19

The foregoing demonstrates the pervasive negative effects of the COVID-19 pandemic on happiness throughout Europe. Ultimately, the pandemic had severe but temporary impacts on happiness, and thankfully, the pandemic seems largely to be a thing of the past. The most recent wave peaked in December 2021, and was markedly less severe than its predecessor, and on May 5, 2023, the World Health Organization downgraded the pandemic.

7 Summary and Conclusions

The Happiness Revolution is alive and well in Europe. Its origins, like those of its predecessors, the Industrial and Demographic Revolutions, lie in a breakthrough in modern science, in this case, the emergence of the social sciences. In Northern and Western Europe, where the Happiness Revolution got started over a century ago, the emphasis is primarily on revising and improving existing welfare state policies and exploring new possibilities; in Southern Europe, on continuing the introduction and expansion of such policies, and in Eastern Europe, on rebuilding welfare state policies largely lost in the early stages of the transition from socialism to modern capitalism. The opportunities for the greatest and most rapid expansion of happiness in Europe lie in policies directed toward the needs of those currently in the lower part of the happiness distribution, largely persons of lower SES.

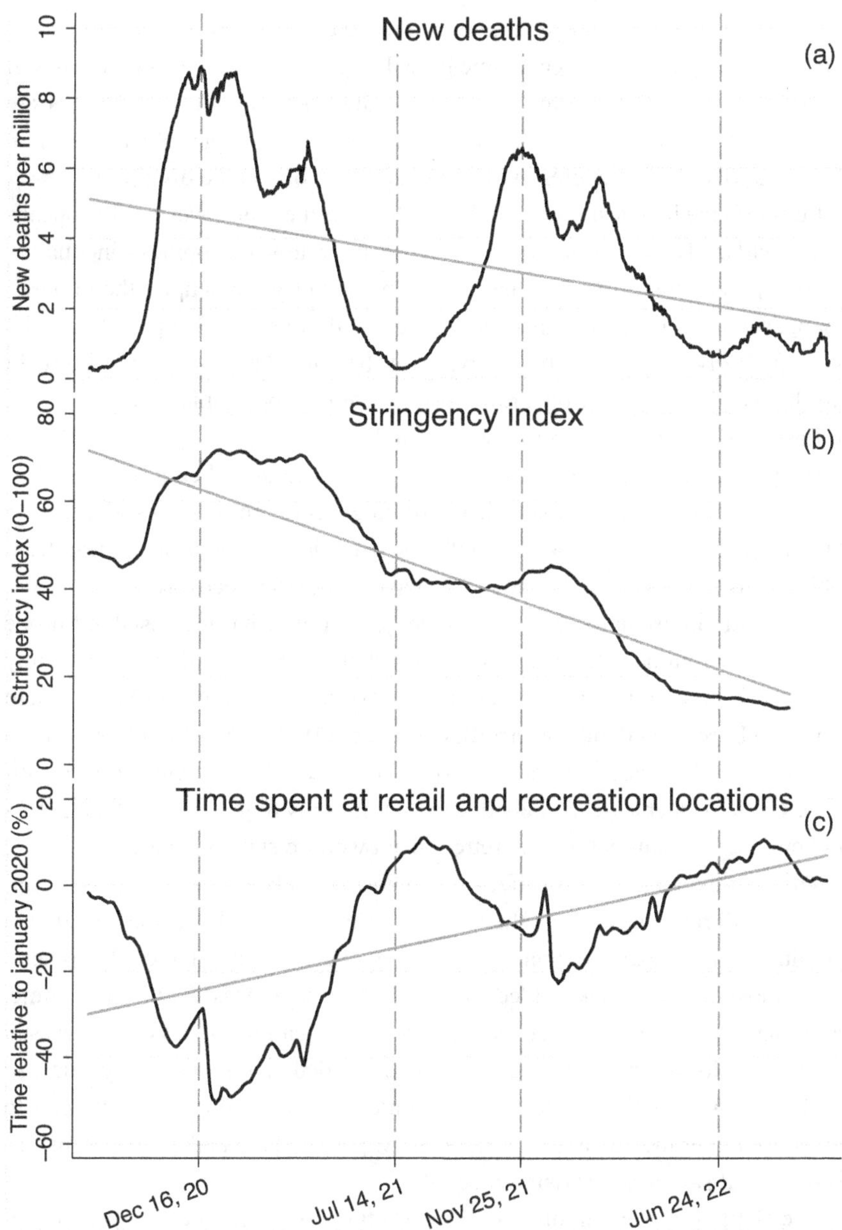

Figure 8 Deaths per million, stringency index, and time spent at retail and recreation locations, twenty-five eurobarometer countries, second and third COVID-19 waves.

Note: Seven day moving average centered, with OLS trend line added. The vertical dashed lines denote the peaks and troughs of the New Deaths series.

Source: Author calculations, *Our World in Data* (Mathieu et al., 2022).

Both at the personal and governmental level there is an illusion that the path to increasing happiness is via economic growth, that is, through raising incomes. It is true that at a point in time if only real GDP per capita and happiness are compared, then countries with higher income tend to be happier. But as shown in Section 3, over time, the presumptive causal effect of income disappears.

Europe is the happiest region in the world – Northern and Western Europeans in particular. These countries also tend to have lower happiness inequality. Among population groups, richer people in a country are happier than poorer, younger women happier than younger men, and older men happier than older women. Native born persons are typically happier than the foreign born. In Northern and Western Europe, rural residents tend to be happier than urban, but in Eastern Europe it is the other way around.

Happiness data for many of the Eastern Bloc countries begin in the 1990s, shortly after the collapse of socialism. To judge from the countries with earlier data, the collapse was associated with a substantial decline in happiness from which all of the Eastern Bloc countries have since been recovering.

The most important insight is that average happiness has increased in Europe over the past four decades in conjunction with the expansion of the social safety net. We observe an increase in Europe, on average, especially in Western and Southern Europe, and the Eastern Bloc (since the 1990s). Northern Europe is an exception to this general trend, experiencing relatively little change in happiness. The lack of change is likely due to their initially higher levels of happiness and ongoing reexamination and retreat from welfare state policies.

The best explanation for differing happiness trends among European countries is different changes in their social safety nets and income inequality. Countries that expanded their social safety nets increased their happiness, while those that cut back tended to reduce their happiness. At the same time, countries that had smaller increases in income inequality had larger increases in happiness. Not surprisingly, countries that expanded their social safety nets also tended to have smaller increases in income inequality. While people tend to adjust to higher income and life expectancy, people do not adapt to expansions in the social safety net or rising inequality.

The Happiness Revolution has a bright future. To date, nine European countries explicitly aim to use well-being in their policy decision-making, three in the Eastern Bloc (Latvia, Poland, and Slovenia) and six in the Western Bloc (France, Finland, Ireland, Italy, Netherlands, and Sweden) (Mahoney, 2023). The governments use a broader set of well-being indicators than happiness alone, but the distinction is not very important here as the spirit is the same. One of the most ambitious goals is to organize government activities according to a well-being framework, in which civil servants would coordinate separate targets (e.g., employment and production emissions) in an integrated system to account for tradeoffs, synergies, and their ultimate impacts on well-being. The United Kingdom has a narrower, yet highly developed practice, in which they expanded their cost-benefit analysis for potential policies to include happiness costs and benefits (when necessary) (MacLennan and Stead, 2021; Treasury, 2018). A further seven countries have new frameworks in place to monitor and report well-being: Austria, Belgium, Germany, Norway, Portugal, Spain, and Switzerland (Mahoney, 2023). This monitoring is fairly involved and typically includes the development of a unique well-being framework, in consultation with various stakeholders, to reflect their population-specific needs. Including both policy-applications and monitoring, seventeen of thirty-seven European countries have so far taken up the well-being banner, and the rate of take-up is increasing over time (for further details see (Brandt et al., 2022; Mahoney, 2023; Stiglitz et al., 2018)). These initiatives represent a further, though as of yet incomplete, shift in priorities from the markers of the Industrial and Demographic Revolutions (i.e., GDP pc, and life expectancy) toward happiness.

References

Alesina, A., Di Tella, R., MacCulloch, R., 2004. Inequality and happiness: Are Europeans and Americans different? J Public Econ 88, 2009–2042. https://doi.org/10.1016/j.jpubeco.2003.07.006.

Angelini, V., Cavapozzi, D., Corazzini, L., Paccagnella, O., 2014. Do danes and italians rate life satisfaction in the same way? Using vignettes to correct for individual-specific scale biases. Oxf Bull Econ Stat 76, 643–666. https://doi.org/10.1111/obes.12039.

Aristotle, 2012. Nicomachean Ethics. University of Chicago Press.

Bartolini, S., Bilancini, E., 2010. If not only GDP, what else? Using relational goods to predict the trends of subjective well-being. Int Rev Econ 57, 199–213. https://doi.org/10.1007/s12232-010-0098-1.

Bartolini, S., Sarracino, F., 2014. Happy for how long? How social capital and economic growth relate to happiness over time. Ecol Econ 108, 242–256. https://doi.org/10.1016/j.ecolecon.2014.10.004.

Beine, M., Docquier, F., Özden, Ç., 2011. Diasporas. J Dev Econ 95, 30–41. https://doi.org/10.1016/j.jdeveco.2009.11.004.

Benjamin, D. J., Cooper, K., Heffetz, O., Kimball, M. S., Zhou, J., 2023. Adjusting for Scale-use Heterogeneity in Self-reported Well-being, NBER Working Paper Series 31728.

Bertrand, M., Mullainathan, S., 2001. Do people mean what they say? Implications for subjective survey data. Amer Econ Rev 91, 67–72.

Blanchflower, D. G., Bell, D. N. F., Montagnoli, A., Moro, M., 2014. The happiness trade-off between unemployment and inflation. J Money Credit Bank 46, 117–141. https://doi.org/10.1111/jmcb.12154.

Blanchflower, D. G., Bryson, A., 2022. The Female Happiness Paradox, NBER Working Paper Series 29893.

Blanchflower, D. G., Oswald, A. J., 2008. Is well-being U-shaped over the life cycle? Soc Sci Med 66, 1733–1749. https://doi.org/10.1016/j.socscimed.2008.01.030.

Bolt, J., Inklaar, R., de Jong, H., van Zanden, J. L., 2018. Maddison Project Database, version 2018.

Bond, T. N., Lang, K., 2019. The sad truth about happiness scales. J Polit Econ 127, 1629–1640. https://doi.org/10.1086/701679.

Bradburn, N. M., 1969. The Structure of Psychological Well-Being. Aldine, Chicago.

Brandt, N., Exton, C., Fleischer, L., 2022. Well-being at the heart of policy: Lessons from national initiatives around the OECD, Forum for a New Economy No 1.

Burger, M. J., Morrison, P. S., Hendriks, M., Hoogerbrugge, M. M., 2020. Urban-rural happiness differentials across the world, in Helliwell, J. F., Layard, R., Sachs, J. D., De Neve, J.-E. (Eds.), World Happiness Report 2020. Sustainable Development Solutions Network, New York.

Cantril, H., 1965. The Pattern of Human Concerns. Rutgers University Press, New Brunswick.

Carr, E., Chung, H., 2014. Job insecurity and life satisfaction: The moderating influence of labour market policies across Europe. J Eur Soc Policy 24, 383–399. https://doi.org/10.1177/0958928714538219.

Chen, L. Y., Oparina, E., Powdthavee, N., Srisuma, S., 2022. Robust ranking of happiness outcomes: A median regression perspective. J Econ Behav Organ 200, 672–686. https://doi.org/10.1016/j.jebo.2022.06.010.

Clark, A. E., 2018. Four decades of the economics of happiness: Where next? Rev Income Wealth 64, 245–269. https://doi.org/10.1111/roiw.12369.

Clark, A. E., d'Ambrosio, C., 2015. Attitudes to income inequality: Experimental and survey evidence, in Atkinson, A. B., Bourguignon, F. (Eds.), Handbook of Income Distribution. Elsevier, Amsterdam pp. 1147–1208.

Clark, A. E., Flèche, S., Senik, C., 2014. The great happiness moderation, in Clark, A. W., Senik, C. (Eds.), Happiness and Economic Growth: Lessons from Developing Countries. Oxford University Press, Oxford, pp. 32–139.

Clark, A.E., Flèche, S., Senik, C., 2016. Economic growth evens out happiness: Evidence from six surveys. Rev Income Wealth 62, 405–419.

Clark, A. E., Lepinteur, A., 2022. Pandemic policy and life satisfaction in Europe. Rev Income Wealth 68, 393–408. https://doi.org/10.1111/roiw.12554.

Clark, A. E., Senik, C., 2010. Who compares to whom? The anatomy of income comparisons in Europe. Econ J 120, 573–594. https://doi.org/10.1111/j.1468-0297.2010.02359.x.

Clemens, M. A., 2011. Economics and emigration: Trillion-dollar bills on the sidewalk? J Econ Perspectives 25(3), 83–106. https://doi.org/10.1257/jep.25.3.83.

De Grip, A., Lindeboom, M., Montizaan, R., 2012. Shattered dreams: The effects of changing the pension system late in the game. Econ J 122, 1–25. https://doi.org/10.1111/j.1468-0297.2011.02486.x.

Delhey, J., Dragolov, G., 2014. Why inequality makes europeans less happy: The role of distrust, status anxiety, and perceived conflict. Eur Sociol Rev 30, 151–165. https://doi.org/10.1093/esr/jct033.

Delhey, J., Kohler, U., 2011. Is happiness inequality immune to income inequality? New evidence through instrument-effect-corrected standard deviations. Soc Sci Res 40, 742–756. https://doi.org/10.1016/j.ssresearch.2010.12.004.

Di Tella, R., MacCulloch, R. J., Oswald, A. J., 2003. The macroeconomics of happiness. Rev Econ Stat 85, 809–827. https://doi.org/10.1162/003465303772815745.

Di Tella, R., MacCulloch, R. J., Oswald, A. J., 2001. Preferences over inflation and unemployment: Evidence from surveys of happiness. Amer Econ Rev 91, 335–341.

Diener, E., Emmons, R. A., Larsen, R. J., Griffin, S., 1985. The satisfaction with life scale. J Pers Assess 49, 71–75.

Dustmann, C., Schönberg, U., Stuhler, J., 2016. The impact of immigration: Why do studies reach such different results? J Econ Perspectives 30, 31–56.

Easterlin, R. A., 2017. Paradox lost? Rev Behav Econ 4, 311–339. https://doi.org/10.1561/105.00000068.

Easterlin, R. A., 2013. Happiness, growth, and public policy. Econ Inq 51, 1–15. https://doi.org/10.1111/j.1465-7295.2012.00505.x.

Easterlin, R. A., 2012. Cross-sections are history. Popul Dev Rev 38, 302–308.

Easterlin, R. A., 2010. Happiness, Growth, and the Life Cycle. Oxford University Press, New York.

Easterlin, R. A., 2001. Income and happiness, towards a unified theory. Econ J 111, 465–484.

Easterlin, R. A., 1974. Does economic growth improve the human lot? Some empirical evidence, in David, P., Melvin, W. (Eds.), Nations and Households in Economic Growth. Stanford University Press, Palo Alto, pp. 89–125.

Easterlin, R. A., Angelescu, L., Zweig, J. S., 2011. The impact of modern economic growth on urban-rural differences in subjective well-being. World Dev 39, 2187–2198. https://doi.org/10.1016/j.worlddev.2011.04.015.

Easterlin, R. A., O'Connor, K. J., 2023. Three years of COVID-19 and life satisfaction in Europe: A macro view. Proc Natl Acad Sci 120(19), e2300717120. https://doi.org/10.1073/pnas.2300717120.

Easterlin, R. A., O'Connor, K. J., 2022a. The Easterlin Paradox, in Zimmermann, K. F. (Ed.) Handbook of Labor, Human Resources and Population Economics. Springer, Cham, pp. 1–25. https://doi.org/10.1007/978-3-319-57365-6_184-2.

Easterlin, R. A., O'Connor, K. J., 2022b. Explaining happiness trends in Europe. Proc Natl Acad Sci 119(37), e2210639119. https://doi.org/10.1073/pnas.2210639119.

Easterlin, R. A., Wang, F., Wang, S., 2017. Growth and happiness in China, 1990–2015, in Helliwell, J. F., Layard, R., Sachs, J. D. (Eds.), World

Happiness Report. Sustainable Development Solutions Network, New York, pp. 48–83.

Ebert, U. and Welsch, H. (2009), HOW DO EUROPEANS EVALUATE INCOME DISTRIBUTIONS? AN ASSESSMENT BASED ON HAPPINESS SURVEYS. Review of Income and Wealth, 55: 803–819. https://doi.org/10.1111/j.1475-4991.2009.00347.x

European Commission, Kantar, 2022a. Standard Eurobarometer 96 – Winter 2021–2022: Annex.

European Commission, Kantar, 2022b. Standard Eurobarometer 97 – Summer 2022: Annex.

European Commission, Kantar, 2021a. Standard Eurobarometer 94 – Winter 2020/2021: Annex.

European Commission, Kantar, 2021b. Standard Eurobarometer 95 – Spring 2021: Annex.

European Commission, Kantar, 2020. Standard Eurobarometer 93 – Summer 2020: Annex.

European Commission, Kantar, 2019. Standard Eurobarometer 92 – Autumn 2019: Annex.

EVS, 2015. European Values Study Longitudinal Data File 1981–2008 (EVS 1981–2008).

Archive, Cologne. ZA7500 Data file Version 3.0.0, https://doi.org/10.4232/1.13511.

EVS, 2020. European Values Study 2017: Integrated Dataset (EVS 2017). GESIS Data

GESIS Data Archive, Cologne. ZA4804 Data file Version 3.0.0, https://doi.org/10.4232/1.12253.

Fabian, M., 2022. A Theory of Subjective Wellbeing. Oxford University Press, New York.

Feenstra, R. C., Inklaar, R., Timmer, M. P., 2015. The next generation of the penn world. Amer Econ Rev 105, 3150–3182.

Gallup, 2020. Gallup World Poll, the_Gallup_032720.dta.

Gregg, P., Harkness, S., Smith, S., 2009. Welfare reform and lone parents in the UK. Econ J 119, F38–F65.

Grimes, A., Wesselbaum, D., 2021. The role of subjective wellbeing in cross-border migration, in Kourtit, K., Newbold, B., Nijkamp, P., Partridge, M. (Eds.), The Economic Geography of Cross-Border Migration. Footprints of Regional Science. Springer, Cham, pp. 217–243. https://doi.org/10.1007/978-3-030-48291-6_10.

Grimes, A., Wesselbaum, D., 2019. Moving towards happiness? Int Migr 57, 20–40. https://doi.org/10.1111/imig.12546.

Guven, C., 2011. Are happier people better citizens? Kyklos 64, 178–192. https://doi.org/10.1111/j.1467-6435.2011.00501.x.

Haerpfer, C., Inglehart, R., Moreno, A. et al. (Eds.), 2020. World Values Survey: Round Seven – Country-Pooled Datafile. Madrid, Spain & Vienna, Austria: JD Systems Institute & WVSA Secretariat [Version: www.worldvaluessurvey.org/WVSDocumentationWV7.jsp].

Helliwell, J. F., 2003. How's life? Combining individual and national variables to explain subjective well-being. Econ Model 20, 331–360.

Helliwell, J. F., Layard, R., Sachs, J. D. (Eds.), 2012. World Happiness Report. Sustainable Development Solutions Network, New York.

Helliwell, J. F., Wang, S., 2012. The state of world happiness, in Helliwell, J. F., Layard, R., Sachs, J. (Eds.), World Happiness Report. UN Sustainable Development Solutions Network, New York, pp. 10–57.

Hendriks, M., Burger, M. J., 2021. Happiness and migration, in Handbook of Labor, Human Resources and Population Economics. Springer, Cham, pp. 1–23. https://doi.org/10.1007/978-3-319-57365-6_178-1.

Hirschman, A. O., 1973. The changing tolerance for income inequality in the course of economic development. Q J Econ 87, 544–566.

Hitokoto, H., Uchida, Y., 2015. Interdependent happiness: Theoretical importance and measurement validity. J Happiness Stud 16, 211–239. https://doi.org/10.1007/s10902-014-9505-8.

Hornsey, M. J., Bain, P. G., Harris, E. A. et al., 2018. How much is enough in a perfect world? Cultural variation in ideal levels of happiness, pleasure, freedom, health, self-esteem, longevity, and intelligence. Psychol Sci 29, 1393–1404. https://doi.org/10.1177/0956797618768058.

Howley, P., Waqas, M., 2024. Identity, immigration, and subjective well-being: Why are natives so sharply divided on immigration issues? Oxf Econ Pap 76(1), 1–21. https://doi.org/10.1093/oep/gpac045.

ILO, 2024. History of the ILO [WWW Document]. www.ilo.org/global/about-the-ilo/history/lang–en/index.htm.

Inglehart, R., Haerpfer, C., Moreno, A. et al. (Eds.), 2018. World Values Survey.

Inglehart, R., Klingemann, H.-D., 2000. Genes, culture, democracy, and happiness, in Diener, E., Suh, E. M. (Eds.), Culture and Subjective Well-Being. MIT Press, Cambridge, 165–184.

International Labor Organization (ILO), 2014. Table B.16. Public social protection expenditure, 1995 to latest available year (percentage of GDP). https://www.social-protection.org/gimi/gess/.

International Monetary Fund (IMF), 2020. Government Finance Statistics (GFS), Expenditure by function of government. https://data.imf.org/.

Kaiser, C., Lepinteur, A., 2024. Reversing the Reversal? An Appraisal of the Robustness of Economic Research on Self-Reported Wellbeing. Mimeo. University of Luxembourg, Luxembourg.

Kaiser, C., Vendrik, M. C. M., 2019. How threatening are transformations of reported happiness to subjective wellbeing research?, SOCARXIV gzt7a, Center for Open Science.

Kalmijn, W., Veenhoven, R., 2005. Measuring inequality of happiness in nations: In search for proper statistics. J Happiness Stud 6, 357–396. https://doi.org/10.1007/s10902-005-8855-7.

Kennedy, R., 1968. Remarks at the University of Kansas, March 18, 1968. JFK Library. https://www.jfklibrary.org/learn/about-jfk/the-kennedy-family/robert-f-kennedy/robert-f-kennedy-speeches/remarks-at-the-university-of-kansas-march-18-1968.

Krys, K., Zelenski, J. M., Capaldi, C. A. et al., 2019. Putting the "we" into well-being: Using collectivism-themed measures of well-being attenuates well-being's association with individualism. Asian J Soc Psychol 22, 256–267. https://doi.org/10.1111/ajsp.12364.

Land, K. C., Michalos, A. C., Sirgy, M. J., 2012. Prologue: The development and evolution of research on social indicators and quality of life (QOL), in Land, K., Michalos, A., Sirgy, M. (Eds), Handbook of Social Indicators and Quality of Life Research. Springer, Dordrecht, pp. 1–22. https://doi.org/10.1007/978-94-007-2421-1_1.

Layard, R., 2005. Happiness: Lessons from a New Science. Penguin Books, London.

MacLennan, S., Stead, I., 2021. Wellbeing Guidance for Appraisal: Supplementary Green Book Guidance, His Majesty's Treasury: Social Impact Task Force.

Mahoney, J., 2023. Subjective Well-Being Measurement: Current Practice and New Frontiers, OECD Papers on Well-Being and Inequalities Working Paper No. 17. Paris. https://doi.org/10.1787/4ca48f7c-en.

Martela, F., Ryan, R. M., 2023. Clarifying eudaimonia and psychological functioning to complement evaluative and experiential well-being: Why basic psychological needs should be measured in national accounts of well-being. Perspectives on Psychol Sci 18, 1121–1135. https://doi.org/10.1177/17456916221141099.

Mathieu, E., Ritchie, H., Rodes-Guirao, L. et al., 2022. Data on COVID-19 (coronavirus) by Our World in Data.

Montgomery, M., 2022. Reversing the gender gap in happiness. J Econ Behav Organ 196, 65–78. https://doi.org/10.1016/j.jebo.2022.01.006.

Morgan, R., O'Connor, K. J., 2022. Labor market policy and subjective well-being during the great recession. J Happiness Stud 23, 391–422. https://doi.org/10.1007/s10902-021-00403-3.

Morgan, R., O'Connor, K. J., 2017. Experienced life cycle satisfaction in Europe. Rev Behav Econ 4, 371–396. https://doi.org/10.1561/105.00000070.

Nikolova, M., 2016. Minding the happiness gap: Political institutions and perceived quality of life in transition. Eur J Polit Econ 45, 129–148. https://doi.org/10.1016/j.ejpoleco.2016.07.008.

O'Connor, K. J., 2020. The effect of immigration on natives' well-being in the European Union. J Econ Behav Organ 180, 257–274. https://doi.org/10.1016/j.jebo.2020.10.006.

O'Connor, K. J., 2017. Who suffered most from the great recession? Happiness in the United States. RSF J Soc Sci, 3(3), 72–99. https://doi.org/10.7758/RSF.2017.3.3.04.

O'Connor, K. J., Graham, C., 2019. Longer, more optimistic, lives: Historic optimism and life expectancy in the United States. J Econ Behav Organ 168, 374–392. https://doi.org/10.1016/j.jebo.2019.10.018.

OECD, 2021. How Was Life? Volume II. OECD, Paris. https://doi.org/10.1787/3d96efc5-en.

OECD, 2013. OECD Guidelines on Measuring Subjective Well-being. OECD, Paris. https://doi.org/10.1787/9789264191655-en.

OECD, 2018. Social expenditure – Aggregated data. https://stats.oecd.org/Index.aspx?DataSetCode=SOCX_AGG#.

Oishi, S., Kesebir, S., Diener, E., 2011. Income inequality and happiness. Psychol Sci 22, 1095–1100. https://doi.org/10.1177/0956797611417262.

Plagnol, A. C., Easterlin, R. A., 2008. Aspirations, attainments, and satisfaction: Life cycle differences between American women and men. J Happiness Stud 9, 601–619. https://doi.org/10.1007/s10902-008-9106-5.

Prati, A., Senik, C., 2022. Feeling good is feeling better. Psychol Sci 33, 1828–1841. https://doi.org/10.1177/09567976221096158.

Rawls, J., 1971. A Theory of Justice, Revised Edition. ed. Harvard University Press, Cambridge, MA.

Robson Morgan and Kelsey J. O'Connor (2020), "Does the U-shape Pattern in Life Cycle Satisfaction Obscure Reality? A Response to Blanchflower", Review of Behavioral Economics: Vol. 7: No. 2, pp 201–206. http://dx.doi.org/10.1561/105.00000122

Sarracino, F., O'Connor, K. J., Ono, H., 2022. Are economic growth and well-being compatible? Welfare reform and life satisfaction in Japan. Oxf Econ Pap 74, 721–745. https://doi.org/10.1093/oep/gpab038.

Sarracino, F., Slater, G., 2024. Social capital and subjective well-being, in Brockman, H., Fernandez-Urbano, R. (Eds.), Encyclopedia of Happiness, Quality of Life and Subjective Well-Being. Edward Elgar, Cheltenham, pp. 180–189.

Schröder, C., Yitzhaki, S., 2017. Revisiting the evidence for cardinal treatment of ordinal variables. Eur Econ Rev 92, 337–358. https://doi.org/10.1016/j.euroecorev.2016.12.011.

Scruggs, L., 2022. Comparative Welfare Entitlements Project Data Set, Version 2022–01.

Scruggs, L., 2006. The generosity of social insurance, 1971–2002. Oxf Rev Econ Policy 22, 349–364. https://doi.org/10.1093/oxrep/grj021.

Scruggs, L. A., Ramalho Tafoya, G., 2022. Fifty years of welfare state generosity. Soc Policy Adm 56, 791–807. https://doi.org/10.1111/spol.12804.

Senik, C., 2004. When information dominates comparison: Learning from Russian subjective panel data. J Public Econ 88, 2099–2123. https://doi.org/10.1016/S0047-2727(03)00066-5.

Sirgy, M. J., Michalos, A. C., Ferriss, A. L. et al., 2006. The quality-of-life (QOL) research movement: Past, present, and future. Soc Indic Res 76, 343–466. https://doi.org/10.1007/s11205-005-2877-8.

Sobotka, T., 2002. Fertility changes in European post-communist countries Ten years of rapid fertility changes in the European post-communist countries Evidence and interpretation, Population Research Centre, Working Paper Series 02–1.

Solano, G., Huddleston, T., 2021. Migrant Integration Policy Index 2020.

Solt, F., 2020. Measuring income inequality across countries and over time: The standardized world income inequality database. Soc Sci Q 101, 1183–1199. https://doi.org/10.1111/ssqu.12795.

Steelman, A., 2011. The Federal Reserve's "Dual Mandate": The Evolution of an Idea.

Stiglitz, J. E., Fitoussi, J.-P., Durand, M., 2018. Beyond GDP: Measuring What Counts for Economic and SocialPerformance. OECD, Paris. https://doi.org/10.1787/9789264307292-en.

Stiglitz, J. E., Sen, A., Fitoussi, J.-P., 2009. Report by the Commission on the Measurement of Economic Performance and Social Progress. Paris.

Treasury, H. M. 2018. The Green Book: Central Government Guidance on Appraisal and Evaluation. Her Majetys' Treasury, London.

Tversky, A., Kahneman, D., 1991. Loss Aversion in Riskless Choice: A Reference-Dependent Model. Q J Econ 106, 1039–1061.

United Nations Population Division, 2019. International migrant stock: The 2019 revision.

van Zanden, J. L., Baten, J., d'Ercole, M. M. et al., 2014. How Was Life?: Global Well-being since 1820. OECD. Paris. https://doi.org/10.1787/9789264214262-en.

Verme, P., 2011. Life satisfaction and income inequality. Rev Income Wealth 57, 111–127. https://doi.org/10.1111/j.1475-4991.2010.00420.x.

World Bank, 2020. World Development Indicators.

World Bank, 2002. Balancing Protection and Opportunity: A Strategy for Social Protection in Transition Economies. The World Bank, Washington, DC.

Wu, F., 2020. An examination of the effects of consumption expenditures on life satisfaction in Australia. J Happiness Stud 21, 2735–2771. https://doi.org/10.1007/s10902-019-00161-3.

Zweig, J. S., 2014. Are women happier than men? Evidence from the gallup world poll. J Happiness Stud. https://doi.org/10.1007/s10902-014-9521-8.

Acknowledgments

We are grateful for the assistance of Malgorzata Switek during the initial stages of this project, and to Giulia Slater and three reviewers for helpful suggestions. O'Connor acknowledges the financial support of the Observatoire de la Compétitivité, Ministère de l'Economie, DG Compétitivité, Luxembourg, STATEC, and the European Union. This project received funding from the European Union's Horizon 2022 research and innovation programme under grant agreement No 101094546. Views and opinions expressed in this Element are those of the authors and do not reflect those of the University of Southern California, STATEC, the European Union or funding partners.

Cambridge Elements

Economics of European Integration

Nauro F. Campos

University College London and ETH-Zürich

Nauro F. Campos is Professor of Economics at University College London and Research Professor at ETH-Zürich. His main fields of interest are political economy and European integration. He has previously taught at CERGE-EI (Prague), California (Fullerton), Newcastle, Brunel, Bonn, Paris 1 Sorbonne and Warwick. He was a visiting Fulbright Fellow at Johns Hopkins (Baltimore), a Robert McNamara Fellow at The World Bank, and a CBS Fellow at Oxford. He is currently a Research Fellow at IZA-Bonn, a Professorial Fellow at UNU-MERIT (Maastricht University), a member of the Scientific Advisory Board of the (Central) Bank of Finland, and a Senior Fellow of the ESRC Peer Review College. He was a visiting scholar at the University of Michigan, ETH, USC, Bonn, UCL, Stockholm, IMF, World Bank, and the European Commission. From 2009 to 2014, he was seconded as Senior Economic Advisor/SRF to the Chief Economist of the UK's Department for International Development. He received his Ph.D. from the University of Southern California (Los Angeles) in 1997, where he was lucky enough to learn about institutions from Jeff Nugent and Jim Robinson and (more than) happy to be Dick Easterlin's RA. He is the editor in chief of Comparative Economic Studies, the journal of the Association for Comparative Economic Studies.

About the Series

This Element series provides authoritative, up-to-date reviews of core topics and recent developments in the field with particular emphasis on structural, policy and political economy issues. State-of-the-art contributions explore topics such as labour mobility, the euro crisis, Brexit, immigration, inequality, international trade, unemployment, climate change policy, and more.

Cambridge Elements

Economics of European Integration

Elements in the Series

The Road to Monetary Union
Richard Pomfret

Completing a Genuine Economic and Monetary Union
Iain Begg

Europe and the Transformation of the Irish Economy
John FitzGerald and Patrick Honohan

The Happiness Revolution in Europe
Richard Ainley Easterlin and Kelsey James O'Connor

A full series listing is available at www.cambridge.org/EEI

Printed by Integrated Books International,
United States of America